Guiding the Plot

Wor(l)ds of Change
Latin American and Iberian Literature

Kathleen March
General Editor

Vol. 20

PETER LANG
New York • Washington, D.C./Baltimore
Bern • Frankfurt am Main • Berlin • Vienna • Paris

Ann Witte

Guiding the Plot

Politics and Feminism in the Work of Women Playwrights from Spain and Argentina, 1960–1990

PETER LANG
New York • Washington, D.C./Baltimore
Bern • Frankfurt am Main • Berlin • Vienna • Paris

Library of Congress Cataloging-in-Publication Data

Witte, Ann.
Guiding the plot: politics and feminism in the work of women playwrights
from Spain and Argentina (1960–1990)/ Ann Witte.
p. cm. — (Wor(l)ds of change; vol. 20)
Includes bibliographical references.
1. Spanish drama—Women authors—History and criticism. 2. Spanish
drama—20th century—History and criticism. 3. Women dramatists,
Spanish—20th century—Political and social views. 4. Feminism and theater—
Spain. 5. Argentine drama—Women authors—History and criticism.
6. Argentine drama—20th century—History and criticism. 7. Women
dramatists, Argentine—20th century—Political and social views.
8. Feminism and theater—Argentina. I. Title. II. Series.
PQ6055.W58   862'.64099287—dc20   95-4675
ISBN 0-8204-2859-0
ISSN 1072-334X

Die Deutsche Bibliothek-CIP-Einheitsaufnahme

Witte, Ann:
Guiding the plot: politics and feminism in the work of women playwrights
from Spain and Argentina (1960–1990)/ Ann Witte.–New York; Washington,
D.C./Baltimore; Bern; Frankfurt am Main; Berlin; Vienna; Paris: Lang.
(Wor(l)ds of change: Latin American and Iberian literature; Vol. 20)
ISBN 0-8204-2859-0
NE: Wor(l)ds of change/ Latin American and Iberian literature

Cover design by George Lallas.
Cover drawing by Ann Witte.

For Phil, Sigrid and Peter,
and for my friends in Spokane

I dedicate this book to all those women
with the courage
to write for the stage.

Contents

Preface

This book started out as a research project on the dynamics between theatre and political change. I was interested in exploring how those playwrights, who under a dictatorial system of government had provided an oppositional viewpoint to those willing to read between the lines, would cope with a more permissive cultural and political environment. I found that, at a time when the discussion of political issues moves from the cryptically encoded text and performance to the streets, several of the playwrights most successful in surviving the newly created vacuum, or in benefitting from it, were women.

This study traces the development of the work of four better known women playwrights: Ana Diosdado and Paloma Pedrero in Spain, and Aída Bortnik and Griselda Gambaro in Argentina. With the exception of Gambaro, these dramatists have not been widely studied. In recent years, contemporary Spanish theatre has received greater attention in the United States thanks to the seminal work of scholars like Patricia O'Connor and Phyllis Zatlin, and the theatre journal *Estreno: Cuadernos del Teatro Español Contemporáneo*, published at the University of Cincinnatti since 1975. Argentine Aída Bortnik is best known in this country as co-author of the script for the film *The Official Story* (1984). Very little is known about her as a playwright. Gambaro's theatre, on the other hand, has fascinated numerous scholars, and continues to be the most widely anthologized.

All four playwrights respond in more or less veiled terms to the changing society around them. While the Latin American playwrights are more directly concerned with the political realities of their country, they coincide with their Spanish colleagues in their increasing preoccupation with women's issues. They often view social injustice and continued political authoritarianism as a direct reflection of the problematic coexistence of the sexes. The solutions they suggest differ widely. Pedrero and Gambaro propose the destruction of the rigid separation between the private and the public spheres. By

xii

turning traditional women's roles into instruments for political and social dissent, or by making the private, previously neglected preoccupations of women the main focus of their plays, these two authors challenge the distinction between the gender-specific spheres of action upheld by patriarchy. Woman ceases to be *el reposo del guerrero*, the warrior's repose, and takes the sword into her own hand, often without removing the apron. Diosdado and Bortnik, on the other hand, seem to believe that women are served better by the separation of the realms of action based on what they perceive as inherently opposing—though complementary—gender characteristics.

The comparative study of Spanish and Argentine women dramatists highlights the conflict between a dramatic discourse shaped by the traditional distinction between the personal and the public, and the struggle against this separation. Notwithstanding the expected, historically conditioned differences between Spanish and Argentine authors, all playwrights discussed here employ female protagonists informed by the social construct called femininity. They attempt, with varying degrees of success, to break down their confinement to the private realm without, however, relinquishing those essentialist (feminine) characteristics, that, in view of their authors, enable them to subvert an unjust social and/or political order. This phenomenon, also observable in the theatre of Chilean Isidora Aguirre, in the novels of Nicaraguan Gioconda Belli, or in the testimonial narrative of Rigoberta Menchú in Guatemala, has interesting implications for the development of a feminist literary theory for Spain and Latin America, a theory that takes into account the particular conditions in which feminism continues to evolve in these countries. I hope that this book provides a step, however small, in that direction.

Chapter One

Theatre in Transition:
The Crisis of the Committed Playwright?

Theatre, like any art form, reacts slowly to social and political change. The artist has to find new metaphors to win back an audience distracted by the cacophony of freed voices on the street and in the media. Thus, my inquiry on the bookfair held every year in Madrid's Parque del Retiro, was met with amusement: "En España ya no se hace teatro político, señorita." I had hoped to find there what I had not been able to find on stage: samples of a thriving theatre reflecting the political changes since 1976, and the *desencanto*, the disillusionment felt by many Spaniards after a decade of living under a democratic government. Little did I know then about the seemingly mysterious ways in which the most social of literary genres reacts to political and cultural change.

The transition from dictatorship to democracy, and the ensuing removal of the need to struggle against the institutionalized control of all sectors of political and cultural life, seem to create a vacuum for the committed playwright. Spanish dramatist Alfonso Sastre points out that the four decades of dictatorship under General Francisco Franco (1939–1975) worked like a "motor" which after Franco's disappearance has not yet been replaced by an alternative driving force (Caudet 80). According to actor Félix Rotaeta, "[W]e find ourselves in a very confusing situation because against Franco we lived very well" (Facio 114).[1] In Argentina, the situation after the democratic elections of 1983 was similar. One critic remarked that the lack of a politically or socially engaged theatre in the first years of democracy belied previous efforts to silence the genre (Cosentino 157). Another critic observes an acute lack of direction on the Argentine stage. Argentine theatre seemed to have lost its subject matter (Fernández, "*El país de los dramaturgos*" 39).

A shifting of concerns and a search for new subject matter and modes of expression have become necessary: theatre seems to find itself, once again, in a temporary crisis. Some seek the solution to the crisis within theatre itself. I suspect that actor Facio reveals a principal cause of the supposed crisis when he underscores the responsibility of the Thespian family to offer the audience a theatre responsive to its needs (113).

Striking the chord that causes reverberations in the audience is what critics claim has not happened yet. Some blame the politics of subsidy allocation which make it extremely difficult for work that is controversial or by young, unknown playwrights, to be staged. Sastre criticizes the Spanish administration for its fear of facing the artist's scrutiny: "My plays critical of *franquismo* are subsidized, my current plays are not. . . . Today it is impossible to do theatre without support by the administration" (30). In Argentina, playwrights critical of the current political situation are quickly labeled "anti-democráticos" by the big press. Argentine dramatist Griselda Gambaro remarks on the discouraging absence of young playwrights from the stage, and in Spain Paloma Pedrero complains bitterly about the treatment she received from the big impresarios (Magnarelli 131, Sangüesa 24).

The political opening in Spain (1976) and Argentina (1983) raised hopes in the artistic community that were quickly frustrated with the wave of commercialism and *destape* (gratuitous nudity) that swept theatres in Madrid and Buenos Aires. Cosentino paints a grim picture of the dire quality of the theatrical spectacles offered on the Argentine capital's Corrientes Street in the mid-eighties (157). In Spain, the avalanche of trite comedies and pornography that arose in part in response to the urge to profane themes taboo under Franco, has been followed by the current administration's wish to create a *teatro de escaparate* (showcase theatre), proof of Spain's equal standing with the rest of Europe's cultural scene. Hormigón deplores that funds which should be used for building infrastructure and for promoting the production and distribution of plays, are poured into international theatre festivals, with little lasting impact (3). This fact together with the expressed wish of the current administration's Ministry of Culture to eventually subsidize all theatre, worries critics and playwrights alike, since it seems to foreshadow an increasing intellectual impoverishment of the theatre scene.

The current crisis, for political and economic reasons, has certainly had an impact on the type of plays that find their way to the stage, and, consequently, on the playwrights' work itself. The most recent plays by José Luis Alonso de Santos and María Manuela Reina are examples of the widespread conservatism of the Spanish stage. The few playwrights who profess a critical attitude towards Spain's modern society and political hierarchy are either "de-fanged," to use Bentley's term, or rarely see their plays staged.

At first sight, the situation in Argentina is similar, as far as this can be judged from the comparatively short time span between 1983 and 1990. Gambaro is cautious when she talks about the theatre crisis. She states in her 1986 interview with Sharon Magnarelli that the cultural sector needs time to recuperate from a repression that seriously affected all aspects of Argentine society (113).

However, and in spite of the choir of voices critical of the seeming inanity of Spanish and Argentine theatre after the transition, both countries have produced a considerable number of socially, if not politically, committed playwrights, whose work in some cases has been staged successfully, and in others, remains largely unstaged. In Argentina, these playwrights have emerged from the years of the harshest repression (1976–1983), continuing to reflect critically the changing society around them. In Spain, a new generation of young dramatists has taken up the pen after the turmoil of the first years under the new political system, calling critical attention to issues they consider a holdover from a traditional, repressive society. That some of the most lucid scrutiny of social and political realities is found in the work of women dramatists should not be surprising. New democracies create a space for voices previously silenced, and in times of political transition "there is a general willingness to rethink the bases of social consensus" (Jaquette 13). Having observed theatre mainly from the sidelines for centuries, Spanish and Argentine women dramatists today break the mold, not only by writing and staging, but by bringing new, challenging perspectives to a genre in perpetual crisis, at a moment when this crisis is deepened by political as well as economic changes. Their theatre points to possible ways out of the so widely commented, perhaps even exaggerated, reign of confusion on Spanish and Argentine stages.

Spain and Argentina share a recent transition from dictatorship to democracy, and they also share the hopes and disappointments that accompany political change. Nevertheless, there are some striking differences between the work of Spanish and Argentine women playwrights regarding the translation of these changes into dramatic literature. While the new generation of Spanish women dramatists of the eighties deals primarily with the personal sphere (male-female relations, individual emancipation, sexuality), some of the dramatists emerging from the harsh dictatorship in Argentina after 1983 continue to be as political as before. Unlike their Spanish counterparts, they often attack the power hierarchy, pointing to the general political significance of each individual's actions and way of life. Their theatre tends to analyze the consequences of repression in ways that link gender-related issues directly with the relationship between the citizen and the state. One possible explanation for this distinction can be sought in Argentina's and Spain's different social and political development, and the roles women have played in the history of their nations.

Unlike the women's movement in the United States, Canada, and some European countries, Latin American feminism has never really existed in clear separation from broader political concerns. Jaquette declares that during the seventies, "[F]eminist groups were deeply committed to linking feminist analysis to the call for profound social change." As happened in Argentina, the militarized state's interference in the heart of the family through detentions and disappearances mobilized "marginal and normally apolitical women," thus destroying the boundaries between the private and the public spheres (Jaquette 5-6). The impossibility of separating private actions from public ones is something found again and again in the work of Gambaro and

Bortnik. It is this perspective that forms the point of departure for their recent inclusion of issues more strictly feminist.

In Argentina, the unstable political course from the 1930's to the democratic transition of 1983 has been accompanied by the important presence of women in the political arena. The reasons for the greater political awareness of Argentine women may be found in the early drive for women's education and emancipation in the 19th century, a fairly strong, though upper-class based feminist movement at the beginning of this century, and the mobilization of working-class women through the efforts of Eva and Juan Perón in the forties. Political awareness among women reached its peak with the crucial impact, in the late seventies and eighties, of the movement of the *Madres de la Plaza de Mayo*, whose activities brought to international attention the atrocities committed by the military dictatorship.

Viewed against the background of the country's unstable political course, the relative prominence of women dramatists in Argentina—prominent enough to suffer persecution and exile—brings to mind Wandor's claim that, "[H]istorically, women have been more in evidence as playwrights at moments of social and cultural change" (122). However, their political commitment for a long time did not embrace a specific concern with women's issues. Looking at the work of Gambaro and Bortnik, this seems to be a subject matter only gradually and recently developed during a time when the political urgency was no longer so deeply felt.

The observations made by two Spanish feminists, Judith Castelarra and Pilar Pérez Fuentes, on their visit to Argentina in 1984, underscore the fundamental difference between the women's movement in Argentina and the one in Spain, and are pertinent to the discussion of these differences in theatre. They criticize the political apathy of Spanish women who failed to respond to the coup attempt in 1979, and in general tend to separate political issues from feminist concerns. They claim that, in contrast to the Argentine women's movement, the women's movement in Spain was initially defined in terms of very narrowly focused issues, like divorce and abortion (Feijoó and Jelin, "España" 43). While Argentine women dramatists in their

6

most recent work take the political as their point of departure and from there approach the personal sphere, several of the members of the new generation of Spanish dramatists (born during the late fifties and early sixties), strive to make the personal political. The differences in subject matter and approaches to it have cultural and historical reasons.

In Spain, the four decades of uninterrupted dictatorship following the Civil War (1936-1939) form a contrast to the political turmoil in Argentina during those years. Particularly concerning women on the political scene as well as in theatre (both highly public activities), the silence was almost absolute. The few women playwrights active in Franco Spain, mainly during the forties and fifties (María Isabel Suárez de Deza, Mercedes Ballesteros, Dora Sedano, etc.), were politically and formally more conservative than the Argentine dramatists also living under authoritarian rule (Hebe Serebrisky, Roma Mahieu, Gambaro, Bortnik). While the Argentines had the benefit of (quickly frustrated) civilian interludes, Franco reigned undisturbed for almost forty years, during which time his and the Catholic Church's conservative views thoroughly brainwashed generations of Spanish women. Though gender discrimination in both countries is still widespread, in Argentina the large immigration from different European countries at the beginning of this century and the melting of cultures that accompanied it, surely led to the reappraisal and questioning of some traditionally held opinions. Franco's politics, on the other hand, pursued the objective of a closed, autarchic Spain, following the historical tradition of a country always a step or two behind the developments in the rest of Europe, a country that for a long time looked towards the past rather than the future. Franco's campaign to ideologize culture while supposedly depoliticizing it, is certainly another reason for the absence of political themes in the work of women dramatists.

With the exception of the plays of Ana Diosdado, who bridges the gap between the dramatists of the fifties and the new generation, there has been little continuity in the presence of female dramatists on the Spanish stage. The playwrights of the eighties have emerged untouched by the experience of dictatorship. Their concerns are new, unheard of in Spanish theatre. Astonished at her not being able to consider herself and her colleagues part of a tradition of women dramatists, Maribel Lázaro deplores the lack of awareness, among her colleagues, of other national and international women playwrights (Ortiz 21). Although they do not always agree on issues like feminism and the significance of women's writing, these young dramatists attempt to close the huge gaps in their history.

Diosdado, a contemporary of the Argentines Gambaro and Bortnik, has been successfully staging her plays since the late sixties. Under a seemingly progressive, pseudo-feminist surface, Diosdado's plays reflect ultimately conservative viewpoints. Diosdado being the most representative woman dramatist in Spain during the seventies—the most crucial time of social and political change—, her work offers an appropriate starting point for a comparative study of Spanish and Argentine playwrights. While the cautiousness of her political allegories contrasts with the daring, disturbing quality of Gambaro's plays, she is one of the very few Spanish women playwrights to address the political situation at all. However, her conservatism regarding gender-role analysis, marks a decisive break between her theatre and that of Paloma Pedrero.

In Argentina, Gambaro and Bortnik, both internationally known writers, have been active in theatre and, in Bortnik's case, film, since the 1960's. Both were exiled abroad during the late seventies, and both returned during the military dictatorship to continue their critical analysis of Argentine reality.

The following analysis of the plays of Diosdado, Pedrero, Gambaro, and Bortnik, explores two major issues in their work: the political commitment of the dramatist, and the construction of a feminist perspective. While we find an increasingly close tie between these two aspects in the recent plays by Bortnik and Gambaro, the Spaniards seem to view these two issues as separate. An analysis of their writing against the sociopolitical background will help us understand some of the reasons behind this contrast. Setting aside the obvious differences between their theatre and its sociopolitical context, one thing is certainly true in both cases: Without necessarily being political theatre, which, in

Kirby's words is "intentionally engaged in or consciously takes sides in politics," these plays contain an urgency that proves that committed playwrighting is not outdated in a democratic society (Kirby 129). In the words of the Spanish dramatist Buero Vallejo, "literature of critical intent continues to be necessary" (personal interview).

Notes

[1]All translations from original Spanish sources are mine.

Chapter Two

Spain's Women Dramatists:
From the Male Gaze to Democratic Alternatives

After a short period of euphoria and politically motivated excitement in the late 1970's, Spanish society seems to be experiencing strong feelings of *desencanto*. According to Edward Moxon-Browne, the "speed with which the transition to democracy has taken place, and the extent to which the process was stage-managed by the political parties, led inevitably to a certain malaise" (20). This malaise encompasses political as well as cultural activities. Monica Threlfall points to political apathy she observed in young Spaniards (56). Moxon-Browne sees lack of concern with political matters reflected in literature and film, where escapism and surrealism seem to dominate over the documentary approach (21). Disappointment in politics, particularly due to the ambiguous course of the ruling Socialist party (PSOE), and in the economic situation, seems to create a climate of apathy reminiscent of the one so familiar during the forty years of Franco's stable dictatorship.

Scant interest in politics and a "do your own thing and ignore everybody else" mentality are also characteristic of the incoherent women's movement of the eighties (Threlfall 51). Women's organizations in Spain have kept a low profile before and after the democratic transition (1975–1977).[1] During the Franco regime, efforts at organizing women, as the one by the illegal Communist Party (PCE), were "not inspired by feminism or an understanding of gender conflict," nor did they invest women with important political positions. The democratic transition sparked discussion about women's place in society and the nature of their struggle. After Franco's death,

> . . . the situation for the women's movement was by no means easy, since opposition parties to the Left now tried to control it with arguments about political priorities, backed by dogmatic analyses that

women's liberation was a deviation from the more urgent task of
building democracy and socialism. (Threlfall 45–46)

Furthermore, the development of a strong women's movement
was made difficult by the "fairly unremarkable history" of
Spanish feminism (Capmany even denies the existence of the
latter), forty years of Franco's reactionary "sex-role ideology,"
and the fact that the new feminism has not been backed by a
democratic culture. While Argentine women seem to have
benefited from the Peronist effort to draw working class women
to politics, the gains of Spanish women during the Republic
(1931–1936) were short-lived. One can hardly expect sudden
changes after four decades of silence, and feminism today is little
understood even by women themselves. In contrast to the
Argentine *Madres de la Plaza de Mayo*, whose high profile before,
during, and after the democratic transition (1983) has earned
them national and international recognition for their capacity to
fuel social change, women's organizations in Spain are eyed with
suspicion. Threlfall argues that the Francoist party's *Sección
femenina*, which served to disseminate and reinforce the
government's ideological program concerning women, made it
difficult for the progressive sectors of Spanish democratic society
to have an unbiased view of woman's organizations. This,
however, is hardly the only reason for the sexist image of
organized women in Spain. In her study of Spanish women
dramatists and covert censorship, O'Connor points out the
cultural and historical factors that have led to cautious attitudes
regarding gender equality. She reminds the reader that current
gender-role division in Spain is based on century-old traditions.
Greco-Roman norms of social conduct, the coexistence on the
Iberian Peninsula of Jewish, Islamic, and Catholic cultures, and,
since 1492, five hundred years of state-imposed Catholicism, have
re-inforced sex-role ideology (1987: 101). Threlfall, who worked
for five years as a member of the Socialist Party's women's caucus
Mujer y socialismo, ends her discussion of the women's movement
in Spain on a skeptical note. In spite of the fact that the 1978
constitution has at least nominally paved the way for change, and
although women themselves are changing, there is as yet little

awareness of the profound implications of these changes for gender relations in private life (73).

The conservatism of many women encouraged by Franco's propaganda machine in the period from 1939 to 1975, and the individualized, very personal vision of women's struggle for equality during the eighties are closely mirrored by the work of women dramatists from the late sixties through today.

Women playwrights, a gender and a genre both silenced in Franco Spain, are uncommon on the Spanish literary and theatrical scene, even after fifteen years of democratic rule. Overlooked by historians and critics up until recently, they fare significantly worse than the contemporary women novelists, who have themselves suffered from long-time critical neglect and reduced publication and distribution of their work (Pérez, Preface n. p.). Evidently, the demands of a genre that O'Connor calls "the most verbal and most public sector of the literary arts" have created even more problems of accessibility for a gender long convinced of the unworthiness of its utterances. Traditionally discriminated against as spectators (banished to the *cazuela* [the gallery] in the 16th and 17th centuries) and as participants since association with the theatre damaged a woman's reputation, Spanish women have either stayed away from the theatre or have conformed to certain codes acceptable to patriarchal society when actively participating in it. Thus María Martínez Sierra, playwright of the first half of this century, hid her authorship behind her husband's name, calling her invisibility "sweet anonymity" in subservience to her husband (O'Connor 1978: 99).

Few women playwrights have become successful on commercial stages and, according to O'Connor, those few have often written from a male perspective, thus following the "masculine censorship code" (1987: 108). In fact, the lifting of censorship in 1978 did not signal important changes for the Spanish woman playwright and female writer in general since she must face the ultimately much more efficient—because invisible—covert censorship at work in the democratic society. The cultural context remained the same: while during the Franco years women were exploited economically as underpaid domestic workers and unpaid housekeepers and mothers with no civil rights to speak of, the abolition of censorship in the late seventies during the so-called *destape* period, brought the commercial exploitation of female nudity into the theatres. Women were talked about, written about, displayed on stage, criticized and threatened for showing their nudity, according to some "an insult to Spanish womanhood" (O'Connor "A Theater in Transition" 205). They did not as a rule stage or participate actively in the discussion on the theatre crisis in this time of transition. O'Connor writes that women, "dismayed in the sixties by the emergence and success of works critical of the values they held dear and shocked in the seventies by the explosion of erotic material", did not champion their own cause ("Six *Dramaturgas*" 116). In 1988, Halsey and Zatlin write that until recently, the most visible feminist theatre is the work of male authors (24). While feminist issues have found their way into the only partially staged work by the youngest of the women playwrights, politically controversial themes have generally been avoided, or have been dealt with in a cursory fashion. In the case of the women dramatists of the Franco era and early transition years (Mercedes Ballesteros, María Isabel Suárez de Deza, Ana Diosdado), this may have been a consequence of the oppressive education that shut women off from public life making independent playwrighting a difficult endeavor, not to mention voicing a political opinion other than the dominant one. In the case of the newest women dramatists, who may have been less exposed to the consequences of this traditional education, one should keep in mind the general tendency toward apolitical blandness in recent Spanish theatre, in fact, in Spanish literature in general. Perhaps saturated with politics in the media, on the streets, in daily life, authors have approached literature as what Argentine playwright Gambaro calls "a place for diversion" (*Lo impenetrable*, backcover). It is also important to remember that the most prolific of the women playwrights started writing after the strongest, most immediate impact of the transition years was over.

In general, women playwrights have rarely spoken up about being discriminated against or being censored, and have not taken part in the controversy about the Spanish theatre crisis during the years of transition to democracy. While there is a significant amount of literature on this crisis, and numerous round table talks have been organized on the subject of continuing theatre censorship in democratic Spain and the difficulties young playwrights have in staging their works, the presence of women dramatists here is rare and sporadic.

Looking through critical surveys of Spanish playwrights, it is difficult not to be struck by the paucity of references to women dramatists. As recently as November of 1989, Ricard Salvat, director and theatre historian at the University of Barcelona, completely omits women playwrights when he suggests playwrights and plays that have been neglected and should be staged as soon as possible. César Oliva, in his *El teatro español desde 1936,* also published in 1989, mentions scarcely a handful of women playwrights, dedicating only six lines of quite derogatory criticism to the extremely successful author Ana Diosdado. He ignores award-winning playwrights Luisa María Linares, Carmen Troitiño, Dora Sedano, María Isabel Suárez de Deza—though he mentions her brother—, and Carmen Resino. Critics of the stature of Gonzalo Torrente Ballester, Fernando Díaz Plaja, Angel Valbuena Prat, Francisco García Pavón, José Monleón, Ricardo Domenech, and Francisco Ruiz Ramón have systematically silenced Spanish women playwrights. Women dramatists themselves seem to have trouble breaking this silence, often even contributing to it. Their absence from Madrid's generally recognized theatres during the time period from 1975 to 1979 may have been owing to their long-practiced passive, indeed conservative, attitudes, even more so since most of them come out of the sheltered homes of the middle and upper-middle classes (O'Connor 1984: 9). They are often unaware of this absence, or seemingly unable to point out possible reasons for it. When asked in 1984 what causes the absence of Spanish women playwrights from the stage, Ballesteros (born before 1930 and one of the better-known dramatists) denies the existence of discrimination against the female playwright: "I do not see any particular prejudice curtailing women's advancement in any area. If they can lead a country, like Indira Gandhi or M. Thatcher, wouldn't they be able to stage a play?" ("¿Por qué no estrenan?"

13).   Diosdado agrees that in previous years there have been fewer female playwrights. But she has no explanation as to what causes this absence.   In 1987, during a colloquium for new women dramatists conducted by the theatre journal *Primer Acto*, the rift between the women authors denying the existence of discrimination against the woman playwright (like Lourdes Ortiz), and the ones who testify to having experienced this discrimination (Lázaro, Pedrero), became apparent (Ortiz et al. 15).

Several authors have attempted to explain the absence of women playwrights from the stage, an absence that seemed to become more acute during the first years of the political and cultural transition.   Lidia Falcón, Spain's leading feminist and also a playwright, ties this phenomenon to the financial investment play production requires.   Women playwrights do not enjoy the same privileges male authors do when it comes to applying for public or private funding, and they often find themselves on the loosing end in the struggle against the tightly controlled, male-dominated world of commercial theatre-management.   According to Falcón, the political ideology of a play is still an overwhelming factor: the author should not be too critical of the parties in power.   That is, women playwrights have to conform to certain codes, particularly concerning feminist issues. What the critic praises nowadays are the plays dealing with so-called "human" or "universal" problems, presented from a male viewpoint. Paloma Pedrero asserts: "There is no room for those who choose to create from a committed point of view, without trying to look for the audience."   According to Pedrero, it is impossible, at this moment, to write or stage plays without addressing oneself to the bourgeoisie.   She regards the task of the female playwright as extremely difficult in a machista society that upholds discrimination and inequality (Sangüesa 24).   María José Ragué-Arias, Catalonian playwright and journalist, states even more bluntly that women's absence form the stage stems from their awareness of the insurmountable difficulties they face before seeing their work performed. ("¿Por qué no estrenan?" 20).

During the past twenty years only one female playwright, Diosdado, has been commercially successful.   Nevertheless, in the eighties a handful of new women dramatists have appeared on commercial and subsidized stages, Pedrero and María Manuela Reina being the most prominent ones. The playwrights from the Franco years, with the exception of Diosdado, have been largely silent in democratic Spain: Ballesteros, Suárez de Deza, Troitiño, Linares, and others. While Diosdado (born 1938) and Reina (born 1958) in more than one way follow the footsteps of playwrights like Ballesteros and Suárez de Deza, some members of the youngest generation of women dramatists (born in the late fifties and early sixties) are searching for new modes of expression more in tune with their times and a heightened feeling of self-confidence. The key issue for them is not political involvement but an increased awareness of feminist issues that appear in their plays despite their hesitancy to call themselves "feminist."

A close look at Diosdado's and Pedrero's work will illuminate the ways in which Spanish women playwrights have evolved since the last years of dictatorship. The differences between Diosdado and Pedrero are above all differences of content and point of view. Apart from a few exceptions like Marisa Ares (*Negro seco*, 1986) and Maribel Lázaro (*La fuga* and *La fosa*, 1986), women playwrights in Spain have not shown much interest in experimentation with form. The ones who challenge the male-dominated canon do so by presenting alternative perspectives on age-old themes, or by addressing issues never or rarely presented on the Spanish stage. Reina, whose plays have approached or surpassed Pedrero's in visibility, is a conservative playwright, with little innovation both in form and content (López Negrín 30). The commercially much less prominent Resino and Pombo, on the other hand, offer a refreshing change of perspective with plays like Resino's *Ultimar detalles* [The Finishing Touch] (1984), *Nueva historia de la princesa y el dragón* [The New Story of the Princess and the Dragon] (1989), and Pombo's *Una comedia de encargo* [A Commissioned Play] (1984) and *Isabel* (1989). All of these are plays with a strong feminist message. In *Nueva historia*, Resino questions the role assigned to women in a society as rigidly patriarchal as feudal Japan. In her introduction to the play, Resino writes that the plot centers on the story of a woman, the princess Wu-Tso, who rejects the role assigned to her by tradition, and undertakes a quest for power. The disquieting contrast between Wu-Tso's fragile appearance and her inner and physical strength, questions our own preconceived notions of masculinity and femininity. Wu-Tso dies on the emperor's throne, and is honored accordingly after her death. Pombo's *Isabel* is the monologue of a housewife who has seen all her dreams destroyed in a marriage that has made her unhappy. Her most recent play, *No nos escribas más canciones* [Don't Write Us Any More Songs] (1990), contains a renunciation of the money-oriented, fast-paced society in favour of a quieter way of life. These plays mirror the flaws of a society in which many are disadvantaged, marginalized, disempowered. The frustration or anger of their female protagonists is a political commentary in itself. These plays express a deep dissatisfaction with post-Franco Spain where the rhetoric of socialism has in many instances not been followed by concrete changes. Plays like *Una comedia de encargo* and Resino's *Auditorio* (no date) and *La recepción* (1994) also attack the cultural vacuum the Spanish stage currently seems to find itself in. They criticize the commercialism of theatre and art in today's democratic society and the sell-out of the artist's creative identity.

The relative explosion of women playwrights during the eighties and their treatment of the themes outlined above—rather the rule than the exception—is not completely unexpected. Diosdado's theatre, still anchored in the playwrighting tradition of the forties and fifties (Ballesteros, Suárez de Deza, Sedano) also departs from this tradition, issuing a critical view of modern consumerist society and allowing at least cosmetic changes in the image of traditional womanhood. Diosdado thus forms a link between the conservative playwrights of the height of the Franco era and the women dramatists of the eighties.

Notes

[1]The strictly political events that define Spanish democratic transition are Franco's death in November of 1975, and the first democratic elections in June of 1977.

Chapter Three

Ana Diosdado:
Theatre for a Society in Transition

Diosdado is by now a veteran on the Spanish stage. She started her successful playwrighting career in 1970, with the staging of *Olvida los tambores* and, with the exception of a six-year interruption (1977-1983), has seen her plays produced in a continuous fashion.[1] Like most of the Spanish women dramatists before her, Diosdado grew up in a well-situated family with close ties to the theatre world.[2]

On a superficial level, Diosdado's plays signal a break with the work by women playwrights of the forties and fifties, both in terms of content and in terms of visibility. Unlike the escapist and/or conformist tendencies of some of the better known women playwrights of the Franco era,[3] Diosdado's theatre contains a debate of some of the important issues of its time: personal freedom, generational conflict, consumerism, political dogmatism, etc.. However, in spite of the relevance of the topics, her theatre seldom attempts to disquiet or disrupt the self-satisfied upper-middle class to which it is addressed. The critical potential more often than not is misunderstood, or disappears under the polished quality of the "pièce bien faite." Part of the secret of Diosdado's success lies precisely in the progressive gloss-over of her plays, which fulfill perfectly well the expectations of the traditional theatre-goers in a society that may have been changing too hastily on the surface for those changes to be profound.

Issues reflective of the social and political reality, and changing gender relations appear in Diosdado's theatre. *El okapi* (published 1974) contains a more or less veiled allusion to the conflict between Nationalist and Republican Spain, and *Y de Cachemira, chales* [And Shawls from Cashmere] (published 1983) and *Cuplé* (published 1986) mirror the chaotic situation in a fledgling young democracy. Although Diosdado does not

18

consider herself a feminist, she does at times voice concerns similar to those expressed by feminists. *Olvida los tambores* [Forget the Drums] (published 1972) implies a somewhat ambiguous critique of traditional marriage, and *Usted también puede disfrutar de Ella* [You Too can Enjoy Her] (published 1975) deals with the exploitation of the female body by consumerist/capitalist interests. *Anillos de oro* [Gold Bands], the popular TV-series from 1983, features the woman professional of the eighties. In all cases, the dramatist's ultimately conservative viewpoint regarding women's roles is barely concealed. The attempt at critical gender-role analysis disappears completely in *Camino de plata* [Silvery Path] (staged 1986), according to O'Connor "the most eloquent denial to date of Diosdado's feminism" (O'Connor 1987: 383). Even *Los ochenta son nuestros* [The Eighties Belong To Us] (staged 1988), a portrayal of the existential anguish suffered by a group of upper middle-class youths during the eighties, makes a sharp distinction between male and female spheres, contrasting female emotionality and intuition with the male concern for sociopolitical analysis and intellectual pursuits. While the issues addressed mirror a society in transition, it may be difficult for some to accept the implicit social criticism in plays where this critique is consistently undermined by the ultimately traditional portrayal of gender roles. This is particularly so since the plot in almost all plays centers around a male-female relationship.

It seems to be precisely the combination of the comment on the hopes and perils of a society in transition from dictatorship to democracy, and the holdover of traditional role-models that has made Diosdado's theatre so palatable for large audiences. This formula, together with the highly entertaining nature of her work and the sleekness of its structure, make the appeal of Diosdado's theatre in some respects similar to that of the work of Antonio Buero Vallejo. While Buero Vallejo is politically more critical than Diosdado, his successful career during the Franco years, and his traditional views particularly regarding male-female relationships, have made him attractive to an audience nostalgic for a Spain long past, inclined rather to hear the familiar critic than to confront the unsettling, unfamiliar voices of the new playwrights.

✄

Olvida los tambores, staged in 1970, casts a critical look at ideological dogmatism, and underlines the unrealistic nature of moral and political idealism when applied to everyday living. The play contains a plea for greater tolerance and communication. Although it is Diosdado's first staged play, it combines some of the basic characteristics of her later work, the most important ones being its progressive exterior and traditionalist underpinnings.

Tony and Alicia are the stereotypical progressives of the sixties. They are married but live in different apartments. Tony is a composer of popular protest songs. Alicia works in a boutique and in her free time practices yoga. They are at odds with Alicia's sister Pili and her husband Lorenzo, a stout and unyielding conservative. In the course of this two-act play the ideals of the characters are shattered: Pili, who has left her husband, reveals the affair she has had with Tony; Lorenzo, unable to accept this, commits suicide.

Tony's and Alicia's lifestyle is almost a caricature of the alternative lifestyles imported into Spain from abroad during the "apertura," the gradual opening of Spain to foreign investment and tourism in the sixties. Neither this type of relationship, nor the exaggeratedly conservative marriage between Pili and Lorenzo survive untouched by the events in the play. In the "autocrítica" introducing the play, Diosdado writes that she attempted to write an "objective" play, in which two characters, the progressive and the conservative get a chance to defend their viewpoints (3). However, Tony's views are ultimately as conservative as Lorenzo's. Both characters share sometimes blatant, sometimes subtle, condescending attitudes towards women, which in their essence remain unquestioned.

The conflict in this play is a conflict between males, because Tony and Lorenzo are the ones embodying supposedly opposing ideologies. The women react rather than act. They do not develop perspectives of their own, and only from time to time, led by instinct rather than understanding, do they question the male ideologies.

Alicia is described as the typical "child-woman":petite, charming, mischievous, although at times sweet and thoughtful (p. 11). Tony, on the other hand, is a reflective human being, "discontented with everything around him, and in continuous struggle with his environment and his own doubts" (p. 12). When Alicia explains to Tony how she became interested in yoga, she sits on his lap, combs his hair and fixes his tie, the stage directions indicate that her tone of voice becomes *"even more"* childlike (emphasis added) (p. 14). Since there was no indication of her speaking in a childlike manner before, this leads the reader to think that Alicia not only looks like a girl, but also always talks like one. When Tony asks her if she is all right, Alicia responds "with the impatience of a spoiled girl" (p. 15).

Alicia does not have a way with words like Tony. When she tries to explain something to him, she gets lost and has to stop, unable to communicate her opinions (19).

Neither Pili nor Alicia are able to use the language of ideology they overheard from their husbands. They are unable to communicate their doubts and problems to each other because they do not feel at home using Tony's "intellectual" talk. When Alicia wants to tell her sister about some doubts she has had about Tony, she becomes pompous in the effort to appear mature (p. 35). She is never able to finish her speech, being interrupted by the phone ringing, and finally by the doorbell. After each interruption she begins her speech anew, reciting it faster and faster. Any importance her words might have is eliminated by presenting them as hollow and meaningless through their pathetic repetition.

When the well-groomed Pili tells Tony's friend and partner Pepe that they have to be brave if they want to create a new world, Pepe's sarcastic reaction shows how artificial these words sound coming from her (p. 39). The play draws a clear line between the male and the female worlds, recalling Ellman's classical distinction between female "idiocy" and male "lunacy." Women have traditionally been regarded as incapable of "impersonal thought, particularly in the areas of politics and history," while men supposedly are more able to abstract and theorize (108). Diosdado shows men to be comfortable with ideological discourse and capable of an analytical approach to society's contradictions. Women, on the other hand, seem to be ruled by instinct and emotion. And even though male discourse is portrayed as often meaningless, it is still the male characters who control the public *and* the private spheres, while women's actions are confined to the still powerless space of the domestic realm. Alicia may be smarter than Tony, quicker to realize where his inner battle between ideal and reality leads him, but Diosdado does not give her the tools to criticize Tony. She will have to wait until the revelation of Tony's unfaithfulness so that she can really communicate with the other characters and with the audience through emotional outpouring. Her attempt to appear "European"—indicated by the stage directions—fails and she breaks down crying (p. 63). Alicia is hurt, but she will stay with Tony, and he knows that. When towards the end of Act II Tony wants to know from Alicia if he can spend the night in her apartment or if he has to leave with Pepe, Alicia reacts furiously, screaming at him never to come back again. Pepe and Tony look at each other knowingly. Alicia's outburst does not mean anything, since soon she rushes into his arms, signalling her willingness to forgive and forget (p. 71).

Alicia is not taken seriously, either for her utterances or for her emotions. There are no textual or subtextual clues that would allow a critical approach to Alicia's image as a traditional woman, just as there are none to permit a critical interpretation of Tony's chauvinism. He does not accept Alicia's pain: she is supposed to live up to his ideal of progressiveness even though he is unable to. He expects understanding from her, and in the end gets it also from the audience. He is able to give a convincing portrayal of the inner struggle he had to go through when he approached Lorenzo for money to invest in a nightclub. Rejected and humiliated by his brother-in-law, he seeks revenge sleeping with Pili (p. 68-69).

Nevertheless, Diosdado caters to an audience with pseudo-progressive ideas when she creates the one-dimensional character of Lorenzo: his machismo is so crude that even the more conservative theatre-going public will reject him. He tells Alicia that he expects his wife to stay home and wait for him with the table set. He likes it when she tells him "tonterías," unimportant anecdotes about the maids, although he does not listen to them (p. 26). Lorenzo is the caricature of the Spanish macho at a time when foreign influence and the first feminist voices in Spain were slowly initiating some change in the patriarchal society. Openly expressed chauvinism was becoming less frequent, but more subtle sexism like Tony's and Diosdado's went undetected, unquestioned, accepted.

ಶ&ಔ

Some of Diosdado's plays can be interpreted as political allegories, although this dimension of her work has often been overlooked. Of *El okapi* Zatlin writes that the "allegorical meaning went undetected, and the role of Marcelo was much misunderstood," basing these statements on reactions of the critics when this play was first staged (1977: 14). She blames this on an excessively realistic staging of the play. I suspect that the causes for what Zatlin calls "misunderstanding" lie within the play itself: the universality of the theme, the conservative view of male-female relations that in a way contradicts the message of the dignity of the human being and his/her right to freedom, and some basic flaws in plot and character development.

In *El okapi* the playwright contrasts the life of the freedom-loving intellectual vagabond Marcelo with the passivity and resignation that mark the life in a nursing home ironically called *El Feliz Descanso* [Joyful Rest]. Marcelo's influence on the elderly, once he himself is confined to the asylum, will outlast his own death: they have begun to take their fate into their own hands, realizing there is a future for them in spite of their advanced age. Several clues within the play suggest the interpretation of the mysterious Marcelo as the memory of the Republic (1931-1939), the seeds of which lie dormant in the decrepit heart of Franco Spain (the nursing home). However, the overly simple structure of the play, built around the conflict between the active male outside the home, and the passive female within, might not invite the spectator of a realistic staging of the play to explore its deeper meanings. The play's critical intention fails because it projects the ideology of Franquismo that viewed women as passive keepers of tradition and as resistant to change, into an allegory about political change. It thus perpetuates the wrongly held opinion that women are unable to be agents of social transformation.

The action of Act One constantly switches from the representation of the stifling atmosphere of the asylum to the adventurous life outside. Significantly, it is always a female character—the crying Doña Teresa, the ever-complaining Doña Luisa, Doña Engracia asking her husband to perform a "womanly" duty (to disentangle wool)—that is juxtaposed with the old but energetic Marcelo: laughing, playing his music, struggling to save his dog, etc. (p. 16, 25, 28, 37). Doña Teresa, Marcelo's counterpart in the asylum, suffers being shut off from the outside world, but her unhappiness does not cause her to rebel; her discontent does not exceed occasional bitter remarks to the nurse and to the doctor, which she then disclaims as "an old woman's nonsense" (p. 37). Her quiet tears contrast with Marcelo's life affirming energy (p. 15-17). His character is further outlined as strong and independent when he compares his dog to himself: he only bites if he is kicked (p. 19). Doña Teresa, in contrast, does not defend herself when other people take away her freedom and destroy her well-being. This opposition between the active (Marcelo-male) and the passive (Teresa-female) remains the structuring principle of the play. One cannot help but be reminded of Yin, the passive and negative feminine principle, and Yang, the active and positive masculine principle, that, according to ancient Chinese philosophy, oppose and complement each other.

The first act ends with Marcelo's arrival in the asylum after he has suffered a serious accident while trying to save his dog from being run over by a train. Act Two opens on a nursing home already completely transformed by what we are to believe to be Marcelo's charisma. The previously stifling atmosphere is now imbued with excitement and enthusiasm. The elderly have become more outspoken and demanding, they organize parties, and new love relationships are established. The actual process of transformation happened off stage, and may be difficult to accept when we see Marcelo's love of solitude and his contempt for social occasions, except when he can make use of them in order to hail the importance of freedom. When everybody in the asylum is becoming excited about the upcoming anniversary celebration for the institution, Marcelo at first reacts with the attitude of someone who feels superior to the childish ideas of others (p. 48). But when Teresa tells him about the plan to ask him to direct a choir for the celebration, he decides to teach the choir members a song he has written about a brighter future (p. 58).

Teresa has fallen in love with Marcelo. Marcelo nevertheless remains faithful to his independence. When Teresa asks him on one of their nightly conversational meetings whether he likes her, he tells her that their relationship is similar to the one he had with his dog. He liked it when he curled up at his feet, and he appreciated his loyalty (p. 55).

Teresa repeatedly expresses her wish to leave the asylum with Marcelo but we know this will never happen. With all her passivity and her inability to rebel, she was born to be captive. She is not fit for the life outside. Thus, in a reprise of Juliet's anxious remark to Romeo when dawn nears, she mistakes the voice of the lark for a nightingale, an error Marcelo is quick to point out (p. 56).

Teresa and Marcelo are presented as opposites not only owing to their gender and the personality differences this apparently entails, but also to their different social backgrounds: Doña Teresa's antique jewelry, her tone of voice, her mannerisms define her as upper class, separating her irreparably from Marcelo (p. 54). Each of them lost a son in the Civil War, and their conversation hints that they fell on opposing sides. Republican

Spain is pitted here against Nationalist Spain. Zatlin draws a parallel between the lack of freedom in the safe and yet confining asylum, and the high price the Spain of Franco's generation had to pay for its isolationist stance (1977: 14).

Marcelo's true identity—that of someone who "for many years has pretended to be a gardener, but has been something much more important" (p. 66)—is never revealed. His death, somewhat surprising within the realistic context of the play because it happens so suddenly, on the allegorical level of interpretation raises Marcelo to the symbolic plane: like the okapi, an animal unable to survive in captivity, he dies, a last sign of rebellion against the confining society he lives in, but also a Christ-like figure who dies to redeem those left behind.

El okapi remains unconvincing on either level of interpretation. It fails as a realistic play on the plight of the elderly because of the one-dimensionality of the characters and the overly simple structure. These are also some of the reasons for its failure as an allegory of Franco's Spain since they make *El okapi* uninteresting as a play, thus failing to incite the audience's critical approach to it. This play foregrounds Diosdado's conservatism. Although she defends the importance of freedom and human dignity, the character embodying these principles is a patriarchal and authoritarian figure.

***

Usted también podrá disfrutar de ella, staged in 1973, criticizes the exploitation of the individual by a consumerist society. Fanny, just a short time ago loved and admired as the promising model who posed in the nude for a perfume, has fallen into disgrace and is abhorred as a monster when several children die as a consequence of a bad vaccine distributed by the same laboratory that brought out the perfume. Fanny regains hope and faith in life when she falls in love with Javier, the cynical writer for a pulp magazine who has come to interview her. When Javier allegedly wants to go back to his wife Celia, Fanny, emotionally crushed,

26

asks him to help her commit suicide. He complies and leaves her in her apartment with all the windows shut and the gas turned on. Javier goes home, writes down Fanny's story, for him an example of the misery of society and of life in general, and commits suicide. Meanwhile, Fanny has regretted her decision and, suddenly worried about Javier, leaves her apartment to find him. She becomes trapped in the elevator, where she is left at the end of the play, completely desperate, imploring Javier to wait for her (p. 78).

For Fanny there seem to be only two solutions: either to start a new life with Javier, or to die. She is unable to manage her life by herself, and when the male fails her—first by leaving her, then by dying—death seems to be the only option open to her.

Again it is the male who is the intellectually active force, while the female is the emotional and passive one. Javier acts. He is faithful to his pessimistic philosophy and ends his life. Fanny reacts. When she finally tries to fight for Javier—though not for herself—it is already too late. Like Doña Teresa in *El okapi*, she is left to suffer.

Fanny represents the traditional image of woman, ruled by instincts rather than by thought, in fact even unable to think. When Javier and Fanny discuss their relationship during the second act, Fanny does not comprehend the things Javier tells her, but she understands, intuitively, why he says them, and knows "that she should continue playing in order to lead him where she wants to go" (p. 50).

Usted también podrá disfrutar de ella seems to be one of the more critical of Diosdado's plays, both in terms of the depiction and accusation of a society based on consumerism and a lack of basic human values like love and trust in each other and in the future, and in the protest against the exploitation of women. Here Diosdado's criticism is directed less against the traditional female gender role than against the sexual exploitation of the fragile, innocent woman unable to defend herself by her own means. It seems to me that Diosdado joins the chorus of voices from the conservative camp (rather than from feminism) that protested against the abuse of female nudity on Madrid's stages, which reached its peak during the late seventies. One of the reasons for

Diosdado's withdrawal from the stage after 1976 may well have had to do with the wave of eroticism and pornography of the so-called *destape* period (O'Connor 1987: 111).

Usted también podrá disfrutar de ella is one of Diosdado's most effective plays. The plot is captivating since it keeps the reader and the spectator in suspense up to the very last moment. The complex structure with its constant shifts in space and time is underscored by a simple stage set that calls for different movable levels easily adaptable to the quick changes the plot requires. The fragmentation of plot and structure recalls the techniques of film making, and foreshadows Diosdado's turn to television during the early transition years.

⚭

In the popular 1983 television series *Anillos de oro* the playwright herself starred in the title role as Lola, a divorce lawyer and what one would describe conventionally as a superwoman. She is the perfect combination of the ideal housewife, mother, and the busy working woman of the eighties. Her role as housewife is still completely traditional. She cooks while her husband looks for an appetizer in the refrigerator, and ends up preparing the appetizer, too, because he is too clumsy to do it himself (p. 144). She mends one of her husband's garments so that he can wear it the next day while he is comfortably reading (p. 154). She loves her job as a lawyer—which she does not undertake alone but in a partnership with Ramón, a longtime friend of the family—but she keeps struggling with the responsibility the job entails. Particularly disturbing for her are the hostile reactions she gets as a woman handling divorce cases. She seems to apologize for her role as divorce lawyer when she claims to be easily intimidated, and not at all aggressive ("provocona") by nature (p. 154).

The television series was launched the same year divorce was legalized, and was thus dealing with a very controversial issue. Diosdado is quite aware of the problems this type of job would bring for an upper middle class woman like herself. She does envision the inner battle of a woman torn between the role most people, including her own children, expect from her—the role as housewife and mother—and the job that interests and fulfills her. Nevertheless, Lola's family life is never presented as less than ideal, and, though she may have doubts about her job as lawyer, not once does she question her role within the family.

In *Anillos de oro*, family life, or at least male-female relationships, are consistently presented as a worthy goal. In the first part of the series (first volume of two, published in 1985) there is not one woman who seeks a divorce out of her own free will and goes through with it. Charo and Luis, after a long marriage without affection, decide they love each other when Charo already has her bags packed. Elsa, the 25-year-old wife of the 60-year-old novelist, Alberto, decides she loves him and goes back to him after a short affair with a man her age who was the reason for their divorce. Rosa loves her paralyzed husband, and even though it is impossible for her to have any time alone, would never separate from him. Alicia only seeks a divorce when she realizes her husband is more than eager to discard her. Alicia's household is the only one that reflects the realities of the working woman in the first part of the script: she is the exploited housekeeper in her own home while she works at the same time as a secretary, a job she needs in order not to feel completely void of identity. Her husband resents that job and wants her to quit. According to Diosdado, Alicia can reach happiness only through another man. The night she seeks refuge from her dreary home in the train station, fantasizing about leaving but not quite ready to go through with it, she meets the eccentric actor and playboy Jorge. He immediately tries to kiss her and, naturally, wins her heart. Jorge leaves, but some time later we find Alicia in Lola's law office seeking a divorce. Lola's partner Ramón comes in with theatre tickets for Alicia. Jorge's company is in town, and Alicia is at the gates of her "wonderland" (p. 306).

Diosdado does defend the right of women to separate from their husbands and she does support women's right to work. But at the same time, she makes it clear that a family or a relationship is more important and more fulfilling than any kind of independence. In the second half of the series, all women not happily married are domineering, unsympathetic characters. The overbearing behavior of Soledad is partly responsible for her son's homosexuality (Chapter Seven); Asun's mood swings and authoritarian conduct cause her husband to leave her (Chapter Eight); the domineering Matilde turned her back on her husband when he went to jail for political reasons after the Civil War (Chapter Eleven). Antonio was thus prompted to look for a woman more caring and family oriented: Concha, "de aspecto bondadoso y cordial," is shown working in her large kitchen or playing with her grandchildren (p. 212, 214, 238). All in all, the message put forth in *Anillos de oro* is the one perceived in Spanish society by a young woman whom Pat Millet interviewed in 1973, and who underlined the importance of being in the company of a male in order to be socially accepted (Beltrán 103).

The script addresses only one issue of women's rights that is not resolved satisfactorily in the script: the issue of equal pay for equal labor. Unfortunately, the short episode in which Lola's doctor friend María demands better pay from her boss disappears among the events surrounding María's relationship with a rich cosmetic surgeon, the accident that destroys her face, and the miraculous operation her boyfriend performs on her to restore her face to its former beauty. María, who at first had regarded her boyfriend as a playboy with high pretensions and few brains, now has to admit she respects him as a doctor, and although she is emotionally completely independent from him and will eventually leave him, she owes him her beauty and therefore, in a world that still judges women by their looks, an important part of her identity (p. 208).

After Lola's husband Enrique has died from a heart attack toward the end of the series, Lola moves in with her mother-in-law. When Ramón comes back from a year of academic and sexual experiences in the United States, they decide to marry, although, according to Ramón, Lola wants their union for the wrong reasons. He tries to convince her that the world has changed, that she is an independent woman who does not need anybody's help, and that she does not need to offer to iron his shirts (p. 345). Ramón, the adventurous womanizer, the one who in ninety percent of the episodes was shown handling the divorce cases in their office while Lola was gossiping with the landlady or preparing dinner for her family, the same Ramón for whom Lola sewed buttons on a shirt (p. 224), and who on one occasion told the concerned Enrique that Lola could wait, "que para eso está" ["that's what she's there for"] (p. 286), is finally the one to remind his somewhat naive wife-to-be of her independence. When she attempts to cede to him the driver's seat in her car, he asks if she does not know how to drive her own car (p. 348). This kind of pseudo-feminism, the one paternalistically granted by men, seems to be the only "feminism" allowed in *Anillos de oro*.

Diosdado appears to chime into the choir of voices that proclaim Spain's difference from other Western countries at a time when the political opening more than ever threatened to engulf the traditional society in a wave of Northern European and North American cultural influences. Thus, *Anillos de oro* contains references to Spanish culture and society designed to boost nationalist pride. Enrique's boss is a Swiss, who finally offers him his position, admitting that Enrique's performance is superior to his own (p. 276). Ramón's assertion to one of his New York girlfriends, "I am Spanish, we are different," inevitably brings to mind the slogan created by the tourism industry under Franco, which sought to highlight Spain's uniqueness (p. 319). The play intimates that democracy will not be able to erase some essential differences, and that Spain is, after all, the best place to be.

⚬⚬⚬

Cuplé, staged in 1986, is, in terms of its use of symbols, the most complex of Diosdado's plays with political subtexts, although it suffers from some of the same flaws as *El okapi*. While *El okapi* attempted a commentary on the lack of freedom in dictatorial Spain, and *Y de Cachemira, chales* may be understood as an allegory of the political transition, *Cuplé* faintly recalls Valle-Inclán's *esperpentos* in its tragicomical portayal of Spanish society after the transition. This "disparate alegórico-festivo" alludes to post-Franco Spain, a society having great difficulties shedding its past and coming to terms with a problematic present, while facing an uncertain future.

Carmen, a middle-aged former *cuplé*-singer, tries to redo her life after the death of her lover, sponsor, and tyrant Pepe, a reactionary businessman with ties to the Church and to the police. During the long years of their relationship, Carmen did not leave her apartment, "buen piso antiguo de oscuro parqué y puertas sólidas" where the dusty plants and the armor in the livingroom create the image of an environment where time has stood still (p. 9).

Carmen and her environment change during the play in an effort to adapt to a new context. Forbidden by Pepe to sing *cuplés*, Carmen now tries to remember her favorite song. After repeated frustrated attempts to sing, she blames her deceased lover for having sealed her lips forever (p. 74). The changes that have occurred in her apartment at the opening of Act Two, are only cosmetic. However, the books displayed are not read, and the armor, symbol for the military, has only temporarily been banished to a closet, ready to reappear at any moment. Carmen, partly a symbol of the old Spain—her name is significant here—, and partly a symbol for the fossilized attitudes of a conservative upper class that hamper the transition to a more egalitarian society, has also only changed superficially. After serious dieting and several visits to the beautician, she now seems rejuvenated and cheerful, and loves company. Nevertheless she still deposits her money into a Swiss bank account and surrounds herself with members of the oligarchy. She dines with her confessor Valentín and with the very elegant Adela, who used to live in exile and now works as a fashionable fortune teller, with several ministers among her clients. The irony is evident in her assertion that all is well in Spanish democracy:

¡A mí me va fenómeno! La horda roja se ha juntado con todas las otras hordas, vamos a reconstruir la patria entre todos, ya no hay especuladores, y cuidamos de las ardillitas.
[I am doing fabulously! The red hordes have joined all the other hordes, together we will rebuild the fatherland, there are no speculators left, and we care for the squirrels.] (p. 75)

Leni, Pepe's young widow, is another product of the confusion of modern Spanish society. She met Pepe when she was protesting as a *verde* against the environmentally hazardous practices of his business. Their marriage exemplifies the sell-out of idealism (p. 46-47). In Act Two, Leni is in charge of Carmen's illegal monetary transactions. The money she is supposed to deposit in Switzerland, she gives to a terrorist organization (p. 95). Ironically enough, this organization is run by Pepe's reactionary sons who, toward the end of the play, blow up one of the branches of Carmen's business. Grau, Carmen's new housekeeper, accuses right-wing terrorists of plotting to destabilize the fledgling democracy in order to return the control of the country to the extreme right (p. 102).

Grau entered Carmen's household to replace the old housekeeper Balbina, who with the winds of change—with the tyrannical Pepe gone—has undertaken the study of history. He embodies the liberal intellectual struggling to survive in a society ruled by consumerism and corruption. A former history professor, Grau now is degraded to the role of housekeeper, a (male) servant to the (female) ruling class. Throughout the second act he repeatedly tries to commit suicide. The last of his pathetic attempts is finally successful when he realizes that Carmen, in whom he had placed some hope for change, is egotistical and cowardly enough to sell him out to the police in order to save her own skin after Leni gets arrested. A love relationship between oligarchy and intelligentsia is not possible. With Grau's death dies the hope for true change, and maybe even a part of Spanish history that could have been had there been enough good will and honesty. This is expressed in the words of Balbina—representative of the working class—who, having lost a tutor, expresses her disappointment: she still has all of Spanish history pending (p. 111).

The structure of the play is quite confusing, a confusion which I would like to regard as meaningful: democratic Spain is confusing. Nothing is what it seems. In the first act Carmen mistakes Leni for her new housekeeper, and Grau for her new confessor. Leni cheats Carmen by using her money to support a terrorist group, and the terrorists betray Leni by setting her up to be arrested. What first seems to be left-wing terror is in fact right-wing terror. The former exile now plays with the powerful. The former maid studies history, and the housekeeper is in reality an intellectual. In short, Spain may seem to be a young, thriving democracy, but in fact it is still stuck in the past and has differing opinions about its future.

While Diosdado attempts a critical approach to democratic Spain, which rather than a profound analysis is a display of its tragicomical contradictions, she resorts once more to the conventional portrayal of male-female relations in order to resurrect the image of the two Spains: one reactionary, the other liberal. Carmen, symbol of the traditional Spain, has all the characteristics that the male-dominated canon associates with the "mistress": she is vain, superficial, emotionally unstable, and definitely not very bright. Grau, on the other hand, embodying the stifled intellectual and liberal side of Spain, is capable of profound emotions and analytical thought. Carmen's frivolity is ultimately responsible for Grau's death.

Diosdado's lack of innovation is also found in the use of slap stick that make *Cuplé* something very close to a conventional farce. Good examples are the mix-ups of the first act, Carmen's open dress when Grau arrives (p. 35), and the black-out scene and the ensuing confusion during Carmen's dinner party in the second act (p. 79-81).

It seems difficult to accept the seriousness of the political commentary underneath the triteness of the erratic plot. And, as in *El okapi*, the characters are too flat to be convincing. The political content of the play can easily be overlooked. O'Connor, for example, writes that the play deals with the transformation of an unattractive housewife into a beautiful and interesting woman, and thus addresses spectators who enjoy the retelling of conventional myths (O'Connor 1988: 40).

Cuplé caters to an audience that does not expect a challenge of its world view, but that nevertheless welcomes a twist of decorative politics, a detached ironical commentary on the confusions of modern society. Diosdado here follows a major trend in recent Spanish literature and cinema, a trend which José

Antonio Fortes—talking about the novel—calls "literatura light" (p. 131).

Ana Diosdado's theatre is not a theatre for social change, but rather one that carefully tests the waters of democracy reflecting only the most obvious signs of the modern times. Her work is cautious, seeking not to displease an audience reluctant to accept social and political change but also cognizant of the need for progressive discourse.

❧

Diosdado is a playwright of crucial significance for the development of a history of Spanish women dramatists. Although she writes from an ultimately traditional stance, particularly concerning her depiction of gender roles, her work in many ways bridges the gap between the stoutly conservative authors of the forties and fifties (Mercedes Ballesteros, Isabel Suárez de Deza, among others), and the group of young dramatists of the eighties whose theatre often deals with the necessity of finding new modes of expression.

Although Diosdado is a cautious playwright in the sense that during her career as dramatist she has been less and less willing to challenge the worldview of her spectators, she did not completely avoid the impact of Spain's political transition and the social changes it implied. New hopes and disappointments have been reflected in her plays. Also, changes in the perception of the role of women have found their way into her work, as for instance the crisis of marital relations in *Olvida los tambores* and the aspirations of the woman of the eighties in *Anillos de oro*.

However, the references to these social and political changes remain superficial. Problems among couples are solved in traditional ways; separation or a truly innovative appraisal of gender roles are not portrayed as desirable or beneficial. The changed political atmosphere is treated in universal allegories that do not address concrete problems facing the young democracy, or if they do, they do it from the detached, comical perspective repeatedly found in recent Spanish literature and film.

Diosdado's traditional underpinnings place her among the women dramatists of the Franco era while the progressive gloss-over foreshadows the preoccupations of a new generation of women playwrights. She is a pioneer in being the first commercially successful Spanish woman playwright to address, at least superficially, crucial issues in terms of gender roles, and to deal with political themes. While treating these issues in theatre, she has not chosen a path different from the one male playwrights were traveling. The treatment of political issues combined with a conservative view of women's role in society is something we often find in the work of male playwrights of the Franco years and the democratic transition. In this sense she is close to Antonio Buero Vallejo, with whom she has been grouped by some critics (O'Connor 1987: 111). Buero Vallejo, like Carlos Muñiz, has espoused a traditional view of gender roles, while at the same time attacking Spain's dictatorial regime (Zatlin 1986: 135, 137).

Thus, one may regard Ana Diosdado as an author who has become successful while, or by, conforming to the male-dominated canon. Her success has paved the path for the newest generation of women dramatists, some of whom now try—often successfully—to break away from Diosdado's ultimately traditional outlook.

Notes

[1] According to Zatlin (1984), Diosdado is the only woman on the advisory board of the Sociedad General de Autores de España (p. 37)

[2] Her father is actor-director Enrique Diosdado, her stepmother the actress Amelia de la Torre. She is married to actor Carlos Larrañaga, whose two adult sons are also actors (O'Connor 1987, p. 112).

[3] See plays of Dora Sedano (*La diosa de arena*, 1952), or María Isabel Suárez de Deza (*Buenas noches*, 1951).

Chapter Four

Paloma Pedrero:
The Challenge of a New Generation

In her book *Dramaturgas españolas de hoy*, Patricia O'Connor subtitles the chapter on the dramatists of the nineteen-eighties with "el reto a la democracia." Indeed, the work of several of these young women playwrights signals a challenge to the patriarchal canon and the traditional views still prevailing in Spain's young democracy. Things have changed superficially, while according to Pedrero women are still regarded as "the warrior's repose" in a predominantly machista society (Sangüesa 24).

The political transition temporarily increased the dearth of women playwrights: the social and political changes shook up the values so fervently defended by the women dramatists of the forties and fifties. The theatre's flirtation with sex and violence in the seventies together with the audience's hunger for sensationalist irreverence drove women playwrights from the stage (O'Connor 1987: 111). The reaction to the upheaval of the mid- and late seventies was slow: while Diosdado seems to have relapsed into more conservative attitudes—her play *Camino de plata* (published 1990) places women at the hearth—, some of the newest playwrights like Paloma Pedrero, Pilar Pombo, and Maribel Lázaro explore themes viewed so far only from a male perspective.

The irreverence of the male-dominated commercial theatre of the seventies, particularly concerning sex and religion, is now found in the work of these young dramatists but presented from a completely different perspective. Their subversive look at themes traditionally in the male domain calls for rebellion against oppressive institutions like Church and Family. Sex becomes a central issue in many plays, either as an instrument of dependence and subjection, or, on the other hand, as a tool for rebellion and freedom. In Carmen Resino's *Nueva historia de la*

38

princesa y el dragón, the protagonist, a Chinese princess, uses sex to attain the power otherwise withheld from her. In Maribel Lázaro's *La fuga* [The Escape] (1986), rebellious nuns escape from their convent in a play where sex has ambiguous qualities, serving on the one hand as a symbol of a newly gained freedom, on the other as a tool to lure the nuns back into the convent. Pedrero, Pombo, and Lázaro view the open acceptance of one's own sexuality as a crucial precondition for independence, thus revealing to what degree the expression of women's sexuality was a taboo during the years of dictatorship. While sexuality is a focal issue, these young playwrights deal with an entire range of different themes, the most important ones being male-female relations, the loneliness of the artist, individual frustration, and the struggle for freedom and happiness.

While playwrights like Pedrero, Pombo, and Lázaro think it is necessary to view things from a woman's perspective for a change, others, like María Manuela Reina and Marisa Ares, continue working from a predominantly male perspective. Reina often deals with themes of universal history, philosophy, and religion, perpetuating, according to O'Connor, "masculine values and gender stereotypes" ("Six *dramaturgas*" 119). Marisa Ares, together with Lázaro, is the most experimental of the women dramatists of the eighties. O'Connor argues, however, that her anti-feminism and her interest in the depiction of machismo and arbitrary violence differentiate her drastically from Lázaro (*Dramaturgas españolas* 52).

O'Connor points out the lack of exploration of women's psychology and interests in the work of the eighties women dramatists ("Six *dramaturgas*" 119). While this lack does not preclude protest against prevailing patterns of patriarchy in Spain's democracy, it may be an indication of how deeply entrenched these playwrights are in the dominant discourse. The rebellion they project into their women characters is often more emotional than intellectual. Women are frequently portrayed as instinctual, given to emotional outpourings, and often dependent on men and on sex. Good examples are the protagonists in Lázaro's *Humo de beleño* [Henbane Smoke] (1985) and *La fuga*, several of Pedrero's characters, and female characters in Pombo's

Purificación (published 1987) and *Remedios* (published 1988) to name a few. These playwrights often walk a fine line between the acceptance of what patriarchy has established as female—or rather, feminine[1]—characteristics, and the use of these cliches in order to subvert the dominant discourse. O'Connor points out in her prologue to Pedrero's *La llamada de Lauren* that women are bilingual and bicultural.[2] They have learned to live in two worlds, and more often than not, have great difficulty to find their own voice. Pedrero has so far been the most successful in putting this contradiction into words and action, thus taking decisive steps in the development of a feminist dramatic discourse.[3]

Pedrero is one of the dramatists who has come closest to finding a discourse that challenges an audience whose conservatism has often discouraged her. She struggles not only against the traditional views of a large part of the theatre-going public, but also against a medium hostile to the aspiring young playwright. After the staging of *Invierno de luna alegre* [Winter of a Happy Moon] (1989) on a commercial stage, she describes the experience as "cruel," and wonders if doing commercial theater is worth the struggle. She is not surprised at the lack of new playwrights on Madrid's stages since the obstacles new authors face when producing their plays are enormous. She describes her dealings with the theatrical management as particularly unpleasant (Sangüesa 24).

While it is difficult for the unknown male playwright to survive on the theatrical scene in Spain today, women playwrights encounter even greater obstacles in staging their work. The independent theatre groups—an accessible possibility during the late sixties and early seventies—after 1975 have dramatically declined in number (Martín Sabas 172). The few that are left often reject the "teatro de autor" in favor of the freedom from interference collective productions offer.[4] Pedrero started her career using one of the few staging possibilities available: her first two plays were presented on subsidized stages in Madrid. Concerning the staging of *La llamada de Lauren* [Lauren's Call] (1985), O'Connor writes: "In order to find a stage . . . she had to perform the female role, direct the production, supply props and wardrobe, apply cast make-up, and do whatever else was necessary" ("Six *dramaturgas*" 118). In her confrontation with the theatre establishment as well as in her critical approach to contemporary Spanish society, Pedrero follows her maxim: "In order to write, one has to live, to struggle against fear and comfort." She has a strong interest in analyzing what she calls the crisis of the relationship and the current return to conservatism. Her passionate scrutiny of male-female relationships offers no easy answers. In an attempt to rid themselves of the ties and limitations imposed by a still-authoritarian society, her characters do not eschew drastic solutions, like the often painful disclosure of a reality that may lead to physical and emotional violence, to separation, and most importantly, to the open acceptance of one's true identity, independently of society's expectations.

In spite of Pedrero's scruples to declare herself a feminist, I do regard her as a feminist playwright since she approaches gender-role analysis from a critical point of view and makes this the central focus of her work (Ortiz 13).

Pedrero, who was awarded the Tirso de Molina Prize in 1987 for her play *Invierno de luna alegre*, is, together with Reina, the most widely acknowledged of the young women playwrights (she was born in 1957). To date, she has staged five of her plays: *La llamada de Lauren, Resguardo personal* [Personal Safeguard] (1985), *Besos de lobo* [Wolve's Kisses] (1987), *El color de agosto* [The Color of August] (1988) and *Invierno de luna alegre*. In this study I will look at all of the above except *Invierno de luna alegre*, including also the as yet unstaged *La noche dividida* [The Divided Night] and *Solos esta noche* [Alone tonight] (both published 1991 as part of a trilogy intitled *Noches de amor efímero* [Nights of fleeting love].[5]

The following analysis focuses on the gradual development of the playwright's search for a coherent feminist discourse and the changes her presentation of women's struggle for equality has undergone. The study centers on two thematic fields present in Pedrero's work: the re-evaluation of the conventional love relationship and the search for female self-expression on the artistic, emotional, and intellectual levels.

According to Halsey and Zatlin, up to 1987 feminist theatre in Spain seems to be mainly the work of male authors (24). Zatlin suggests a possible explanation for this phenomenon: The male dramatists who have championed feminist causes "include some who until the decriminalization of homosexuality in democratic Spain, used the oppression of women as the vehicle for a criticism of machismo that they have since been able to express in less veiled terms" (1986: 134). Interestingly enough, Pedrero starts her search for female self-expression by presenting the plight of a male individual whose emotional and physical inclinations make him an outcast in a society the norms of which are in relentless and unmerciful contradiction to his feelings, thoughts and wishes, a plight similar to the one women have to endure. *La llamada de Lauren* reflects the greater permissiveness of Spanish popular culture regarding male cross-dressing and homosexuality, which, thanks in part to the efforts of filmmaker Pedro Almodóvar, has gathered much greater attention than women's liberation. The play questions the fixed identities society establishes for each individual, and for each gender. It challenges our own assumptions about marital relations, and the swiftness with which we draw conclusions about sexual preference when an individual refuses to conform to the social norm. While Pedrero's first play deals with a man's initial step toward liberation, it foregrounds the link between male and female sexual stereotyping, and hints at the necessary transformation of women's roles.

La llamada de Lauren was first staged in 1985, in Madrid's subsidized *Centro Cultural de la Villa*. Pedro and Rosa are about to celebrate their third wedding anniversary, which falls on the same day as Carnival, an occasion for all to discard their social masks.

Much to Rosa's surprise, Pedro has dressed up as his idol Lauren Bacall, and has also provided a costume for his wife: he wants her to assume the role of Humphrey Bogart. A game with reversed roles ensues in the course of which the frustrations of their marriage and the social pressures that have caused them are gradually revealed. After a violent climax, the two characters have learned something about themselves and each other that will completely change and possibly destroy their relationship.

The play generated a very mixed reaction, divided along gender lines. O'Connor writes in the prologue to the 1987 edition that the reaction of the women among the spectators was considerably more positive and understanding than the reaction of the male audience members (p. 16). Women seem to be more familiar with the existence of two codes: the domineering patriarchal code, and the as yet incomplete and unassertive code of the socially and politically underprivileged.

La llamada de Lauren contrasts the two codes and shows how easy it is for the individual to have a double standard. Pedro's love for cross-dressing, and thus his rejection of the masculine role models, has been brutally repressed since his early childhood. To fit into society, he has adopted the dominant code and behaved according to its social rules. After three years of marriage he realizes he has been stifling his true self, but he is unaware of how deeply seated his acceptance of traditional forms of behavior really is, particularly concerning his attitude towards Rosa. Pedro dresses up as a "woman" in the sense of what patriarchal society conceives as the ideal female: the cliché of the beautiful and enigmatic Lauren Bacall. Pedro-Lauren wants to be seduced by Rosa-Bogart, the epitome of the tough male: "duro y romántico a la vez que profundo" (p. 46). The seduction game they play implies only a reversal of traditional gender roles, not an attack on these gender roles themselves.

At first, Rosa accepts Pedro's transformation and even rejoices at his courage, delighted that Pedro, who has always voiced his loathing for transvestites, dares to drop the mask of the boring state employee (p. 31). However, although Pedro acts like a "new man" in finally attempting to deal with his suppressed homosexual inclinations, it quickly becomes clear that this attitude does not extend to his relationship with Rosa. When Rosa jokingly responds to his offer always to dress like a woman by sitting down, grabbing the newspaper and asking her husband to prepare dinner, he is upset, realizing that Rosa is impersonating him (p. 31). Although he denies that he is the typical traditional husband, his domineering behavior extends into their role play. When a little later Pedro wants Rosa to act like a man and make love to him like a man, she has to follow his rules, and is not allowed to set up her own game (p. 32). Pedro binds up her breasts despite her protests, and asks her to adopt the external as well as the inernal *gestus* of the masculine prototype: "Quiero que modifiques . . . el alma." ["I want you to change . . . your soul."] (p. 37). But when what she thought to be her anniversary gift turns out to be a penis from a sex shop, she is outraged and refuses to wear it (p. 39). She finally senses there is something really wrong, and feels the need to talk to Pedro about their relationship (p. 40). Neither of them is, however, ready to communicate, unable to overcome social taboos. Therefore, an increasingly violent ritual acts as a substitute, revealing the inadequacy and superficiality of traditional gender roles.

While for Rosa the role reversal is a game and gives her a chance to be physically close to her husband, for him it is absolutely serious. The roles they assume in the game are traditional. Pedro is Azucena, a hairdresser who lives with her mother, and dreams of being a high-fashion model (p. 42). Rosa is Carlos, but she plays the role of the man she knows best, her own husband. She explains to Pedro-Azucena the reasons for the break-up with "his" wife, describing to "her" the busy schedule that Pedro keeps in real life (p. 44). She takes advantage of the game to vent her own frustrations in spite of Pedro's protests. Carlos explains to Azucena that his wife, miserable because of his neglect, one day "hizo la maleta y . . . se murió" ["she packed her suitcase and . . . died"] (p. 45). The pause before "se murió" indicates that Rosa really intended to conclude the sentence logically with "se fue" ["she left"], but probably aware that this would be too close to her own experience and secret wishes and could hurt Pedro's feelings, she does not say it. While Pedro is taking a definite step—even though it is the step of the cowardly—to express his unhappiness with their relationship and with his role in it, Rosa is not ready for an open confrontation with Pedro. Desperately clinging to her role as a traditional wife, she refuses to acknowledge her husband's problem. Her initial acceptance of his transformation turns into utter rejection and disgust in the deeply moving culmination of the play. Groping for her role as Rosa, the wife, she attempts to restore the fragile order from which Pedro frees himself by completely losing control. When Pedro forces her to play the male role in bed, her emotions range from initial fear to the final angry outburst that ends their game (p. 50–51).

Pedro's attempts to explain his problem to Rosa fall on deaf ears. Although Rosa probably understands why he is suffering, she is afraid that admitting this would question her own identity. Thus, she belittles his traumatic childhood experiences by underlining their ordinariness (p. 56–57). Her remarks reveal that society has built a pattern of demands and expectations that crush the individual's development and cause the frustrations and anger felt by Pedro.

Both Pedro and Rosa are the victims of a code they have internalized and that is now tearing them apart. Pedro reacted to the punishment by his father by being more macho than anybody else (p. 57). Rosa is crushed by the destruction of her world which, though built on roles and attitudes she herself criticizes, had nevertheless provided a safe haven.

Rosa is the true victim in the game, because it was Pedro's game. When after another failed attempt to be the traditional husband he leaves the apartment to join the Carnival, she paints his lips and wishes him a good time. Misery overcomes her once she is left alone. The old roles are destroyed. While Pedro has found a new role—which may turn out to be as fragile as the old one—she is left without any role, on the threshold of an identity she may be able to build once she has found the discourse to subvert the patriarchal one that defines and confines her.

La llamada de Lauren looks at the effects the pressures of authoritarian society have on the individual, be it woman or man. Although Pedrero wants to make clear that both genders are victims of expectations they cannot and should not meet, it is obvious that the female co-protagonist has greater difficulties asserting herself. Pedro's emancipation is not complete. His image of women is traditional: Lauren Bacall is an image created by the dominant patriarchal code. By assuming this role, he only has proved the interchangeability of the traditional gender roles, but not the hollowness of the roles themselves. The gradual dismantling of these roles and the ideology behind them will move increasingly into the center of attention in Pedrero's later plays.

∾≈∾

Resguardo personal was staged in 1986 under the direction of the playwright in the "Taller de Autores del Centro Nacional de Nuevas Tendencias Escénicas." Some aspects of this short one-act play make it similar to Pedrero's first play. The central theme is again the crisis of a marital relationship, though from a different point of view. As in *La llamada de Lauren*, the author makes use of a metatheatrical device when the female character assumes a fictitious role within the play, only this time this is not revealed until the end.

Marta has left her husband Gonzalo, tired of her role as neglected housewife, useful only as moral support for Gonzalo's career advancement. Gonzalo comes to see her, hoping to convince her to return to him, and, since she refuses, to take back the dog Nunca ("Never") he claims she abducted from his apartment while he was gone. Marta regards Nunca as her dog since she was always the one who cared for her, fed her, and walked her. She acts as if she took the dog to the pound, where she has to pick her up showing a receipt before they close at eight if she does not want her to be put to sleep. Gonzalo, more eager to hurt Marta than to save Nunca's life, prevents her from leaving the apartment. After he has left, convinced that the dog is dead and satisfied at having caused Marta's despair, Marta lets Nunca out of the box where she has been sleeping.

Resguardo personal is about the destructive power of love gone bad. It questions the traditional relationship that banishes the woman to the home while the man works long hours outside the home in order to support the family. Gonzalo tries to explain the reasons for his neglect by reminding Marta of his many responsibilities and sacrifices (p. 101–102). Loneliness and disappointment led Marta to have an affair with a neighbor, and, finally, to leave her husband in order to live alone (p. 101). The pain Marta's affair inflicted on Gonzalo is not so much truly felt as it is socially conditioned. What bothered him most was the fact that Marta openly pursued the affair, without taking precautions to keep it secret (p. 200). In his insistence on calling Marta "desequilibrada" and "loca" ("crazy woman"), he overlooks his own outrageous behavior: he sacrifices the dog he supposedly loves, in order to hurt Marta. Not only does he prevent her from leaving the apartment to pick up Nunca, he even calls the Humane Society at eight to make sure it is closed (p. 104). Like the child in Edward Albee's *Who's Afraid of Virginia Woolf* (1962), the dog becomes a symbol for the fragile bond that holds a relationship together. Nunca embodies the knowledge of each other's weaknesses that, once a condition for mutual understanding and affection, turns into an instrument for the greatest cruelty.

The interest of *Resguardo personal* lies mainly in its significance as a further step in Pedrero's development of a "dramaturgia femenina." Pedrero explores the brittle boundary between love and cruelty, a boundary easily transgressed in any intimate relationship. The diametrically opposed expectations patriarchal society has concerning women and men destroys the respect for each other necessary for harmonious coexistence.

ॐ

Besos de lobo, staged in a theatre workshop in 1987, is the account of a long wait and a final awakening. Set in a small Castilian village in the seventies, this play is reminiscent of García Lorca's rural tragedies in its portrayal of the confining reality of women's lives in a conservative rural Spain. *Besos de lobo* adds a mythical dimension to the story of one woman's journey to independence from society's confining definition of her role.

Ana, the eighteen-year-old daughter of the widower Agustín, comes back to Jara after spending several years in a convent in Madrid, carrying a suitcase full of books. She was sent to Madrid after her mother's death, to avoid conflict between her and her aunt Paulina, her father's lover. Her return to Jara is officially due to a lung infection from which she has to recover, but we learn soon that she lost her job as cleaning woman in the convent because she got pregnant. Ana suffers a serious trauma from this never fully explained incident, which she completely denies (p. 21). As a result of her traumatic experience, Ana rejects male heterosexuality and clings to the traditional role that best defends her from it: the role of the faithful bride-to-be who waits for her faraway fiancé. Thus she fends off all attempts by her father to marry her to her childhood friend Camilo, who is in love with her. Her mysterious fiancé is also the pretext for her not to accept a job as maid in a doctor's household in the capital (p. 10). As a woman with no money and little education, Ana has few, if any, possibilities of being independent: the jobs she could have expose her to sexual and economic exploitation, as her employment as maid in the convent has shown.

Her best defense seems to be staying at home, and even there she is confronted with the male sexuality she seeks to avoid. She blames her father for her mother's death. Shortly before her mother died from a long illness that hindered her from having sexual intercourse, Ana saw her father and her aunt Paulina making love in the chicken coop (p. 22). Her rejection of her father's sexuality on the one hand, and her jealous currying favor with him on the other, mirror her ambiguous feelings towards Camilo. She feels attracted to him and at the end of the play even tells him so, but she rejects a relationship on the pretext of her engagement to Raúl. However, the real reason for her rejection is not Raúl, the man who probably made her pregnant and then left her with empty promises. It is rather her fear of the pain a relationship with the opposite sex has brought her and may bring her again. She is convinced that every contact between the sexes is ultimately reduced to the physical passion that turns women into victims (p. 28). Luciano, on the other hand, is a youngster troubled by his homosexual inclinations and poses no threat to Ana. When he has followed her request and touched her without being aroused, she is relieved: "Me has demostrado que no eres como los demás" ["You have proved to me that you are not like the others"] (p. 34).

Ana and Luciano are outcasts in Jara's closed society. While Ana is regarded as a witch or a madwoman by the villagers, Luciano is judged a little retarded. Ana remarks that, in Jara, being different means the same as being mad or foolish (p. 32). Together they create a world where they can live out their fantasies. Ana is an artistically sensitive woman. She spends most of her time reading and fantasizing. She writes love letters she asks Luciano to mail to her, thus maintaining the fiction of a faithful Raúl who will soon come and take both of them far away from Jara. Ana and Luciano share a sexuality different from the one established as a norm in the society they live in. Nevertheless, social pressure destroys their trust in each other, and Luciano abandons Ana. He marries in order to maintain a facade of normalcy.

The final scene finds her at the train station, waiting for the six o'clock express she is going to board in order to avoid Raúl, who after many years has finally announced his arrival. She tells Camilo, who supervises the station that Raúl's telegram made her realize she did not want to wait another day, opening her eyes to a new, now possible freedom (p. 51). She asks Camilo to come with her, knowing already that he will not be able to accept such a spontaneous offer. After she is gone, "to a place where there is a sea," Raúl and Camilo are left alone at the station, Raúl struck with disbelief, Camilo angry with himself.

Ana has left behind a small wooden statue that Camilo once gave to her. It represents the Egyptian goddess Isis, who for a moment succeeded in reawakening her husband Osiris from the dead to conceive a child by him. In Camilo's carving, she holds that child. When Ana first heard the legend, she was deeply affected by it, probably because she lost her own child. But when she leaves Jara, she does not identify with the concept of eternal love and traditional womanhood anymore. Confident and dressed in white, Ana departs from the village where soon no more trains will stop. Jara gains mythical dimensions as the place where time stands still, where repressed sexuality seeks an outlet in bestiality, where sexual difference is treated with drugs and women wait for years in darkened houses for their forgetful lovers. Ana does not wait any longer.

With Ana, Pedrero has created a character that completely defies her traditional gender role, and in *Besos de lobo*, a play that has all the elements of a classic tragedy but that subverts the potentially tragic outcome by Ana's escape. Ana's final step is not the result of long pondering but rather a spontaneous break with an environment that confines and judges her. This seems to be a characteristic of several of Pedrero's characters who decide to break the social rules before these break them, in an often violent and unpremeditated act of rebellion. It is not a question of good against evil: there generally are no good or evil characters in Pedrero's plays. Ana does not ask for sympathy. She is not portrayed as a helpless victim, but rather as angry and vengeful. She blackmails her father emotionally by feigning seizures due to an imaginary illness. Like most of Pedrero's female characters, she does not want to do what patriarchal society deems best for her. She acts "un-daughterly" and "un-womanly," and is therefore regarded as mad. Ana never forgives what she considers her father's betrayal, and insults him even during his wake. She will not marry Camilo, even though he is friendly, sensitive, and artistically inclined like her. Her refusal to accept the love offered by Camilo challenges the traditional expectations of an audience accustomed to a theatre that sanctions middle-class values.

Although the play's ingredients must ring familiar to a public acquainted with Spanish drama since the Golden Age—the rural setting, the disgraced young woman, the noble suitor—, Pedrero subverts handed-down clichés by favoring conflict solution radically different from that offered in classical Spanish theatre. The powerful father figure, concerned with the daughter's honor according to the dramatic convention of the Golden Age, here is portrayed as weak, and finally dies. Ana chooses to leave rather than marry. Aware of the lack of understanding she would encounter from Raúl, she leaves him a note at the train station informing him that she loves someone else. That someone is herself.

In *Besos de lobo* the men are left behind, defeated, shocked, confused by a woman who defies their traditional expectations. They literally missed her train, one of the last to leave Jara, a village that becomes symbolic for the Spain reluctantly left behind during the democratic transition. Not without reason is the play set in the seventies, a time when the noise of the world rushed through Spain's open doors without being more than a far-away clamor for the more conservative segments of its society.

⁂

The woman as artist, her search for a voice of her own, for an identity untainted by commercialism and the limitations of the patriarchal canon, seems to be a theme dear to many writers interested in a critical analysis of traditional gender roles. Pedrero's characters very often are women artists. Ana in *Besos de lobo* writes poetry and walks around the house reciting it, dressed in a long robe and wearing a large hat. In *Invierno de luna alegre* the young Reyes forms part of a small street theatre, and dreams about a career as a nightclub dancer and singer. Sabina in *La noche dividida* is an actress tired of her role in a commercial melodrama, and *El color de agosto* is a play about a painter who has sold out to commercial interests and now struggles to find her true identity as individual and as artist.

This search for personal and artistic self-expression has long been a subject of feminist writing, at least from Virginia Woolf to Canadian novelist Margaret Atwood. The woman as writer, as painter, as actress pursues only seemingly a double goal. The fight of the artist not to become absorbed by so-called mainstream commercialism is only an extension of her struggle for personal freedom. For Margaret Atwood's Elaine in her novel *Cat's Eye* (1988) and for María in Pedrero's *El color de agosto*, painting is a way of coming to terms with their own anguish, an anguish caused by the fear of facing unresolved problems, ultimately the fear of facing themselves.

La noche dividida in many ways is a link between *Besos de lobo* and *El color de agosto*. While *La noche dividida* deals mainly with a woman's struggle to free herself from a frustrating long-distance relationship, in *El color de agosto* the male-female relationship is relegated to the background. The focus is on the artist's search for her personal and artistic freedom. In *La noche dividida* the metatheatrical aspect underscores the role-playing women are trained for in a society where the dominant code forces them into silence or distortion of their identity.

The young actress Sabina García has decided to break up with her boyfriend, Jean Luc. He calls her every Tuesday evening from France, always promising her he will visit her the following week. It is Tuesday and he has not called. While she impatiently waits for the phone to ring, she rehearses her part in a cheap commercial melodrama. She hates that role—the one of a woman betrayed and then murdered by her lover—as much as she hates her real-life role as the always waiting, faithful girlfriend. Sabina has decided to end the relationship, but fears her own weakness, knowing full well that his voice will silence hers (p. 64). That Jean Luc finally does return to her the keys to her apartment and steps out of her life, is not so much the result of Sabina's willpower, as of chance. Sabina gets drunk together with Adolfo, a young Bible vendor who came to her door trying to sell her one of his Bibles. When Jean Luc arrives after one year of empty promises, he finds them asleep and half-naked on the terrace.

The title hints at Sabina's split identity and her role-playing. Sabina experiences the night from behind a series of different masks, and is only partially aware of her own split identity. Sabina is tired of the roles she has been performing, but she has not found anything with which to replace them. She cannot identify with the abandoned lover in whose role she is cast: "No puedo encontrar realidades paralelas" ["I cannot see any parallels in real life"] (p. 60). Ironically, her role in the play is an exaggerated mirror image of her role in real life. The woman in the melodrama finally decides to throw her abusive husband out of her house, but she is punished for this when he murders her, her last words expressing acceptance of her fate (p. 58).

Sabina's relationship with Jean Luc is characterized by a similar kind of dependency. Sabina feels she is the subject of her boyfriend's whims. Never having made a single decision in their relationship, she realizes she has no control over it. The fear of losing Jean Luc has turned her into a melancholy woman, and "men do not like sad women" (p. 70). Sabina is caught in a vicious cycle. She realizes she is dependent on male appreciation, but also that she does not have the strength to break that cycle. She constantly measures herself according to her degree of attractiveness to the male gender. That she needs to get drunk in order to end a stale relationship, and that she needs Adolfo to stay with her, are signs of her fragility.

Desperate because Jean Luc has not called her, Sabina seeks Adolfo's appreciation in an erotic game in which she assumes yet another role. Torn between her frustration over Jean Luc's forgetfulness and her wish for independence, she seduces Adolfo (p. 71, 72). Her hunger to be loved by the opposite sex underlines her continuing dependency: she repeatedly asks Adolfo if he loves her. Here, the gesture becomes more important than the truth, and underlines the vacuousness of the traditional gender relationship. Sabina's wish to end her relationship with Jean Luc entails more than just the end of an affair. It is the rejection of a type of love that makes her dependent and prevents her from seeing clearly (p. 69).

Sabina's discourse conforms to the dominant patriarchal code. In her attempt to seduce Adolfo, rebelling against her dependence on Jean Luc, she uses the vocabulary that reinforces her dependence on the male gender. Despite her efforts to focus solely on the physical relationship, she talks about love. Adolfo, on the other hand, talks about sex, in an interesting display of traditional behavior, sanctioned by the dominant code. Sabina defines herself by the effect she has on the male gender, thus recalling the female protagonist of *La llamada de Lauren* who blames herself for Pedro's lack of sexual interest in her (p. 53).

Sabina's identity crisis is mirrored by Adolfo's own search for purpose. The fact that he sells Bibles hints at the meaninglessness of a value system once hailed as essential for the moral—though not economic—benefit of society. Pedrero draws a parallel between Adolfo and Sabina, just as she did in *Besos de lobo* between Ana and Luciano. She seems to imply that the fate of women is similar to the fate of other marginalized individuals in modern Spanish society: the urban poor in *La noche dividida, Solos esta noche* and *Invierno de luna alegre,* and the homosexual in *La llamada de Lauren* and *Besos de lobo.*[6]

Like many of Pedrero's characters, Sabina is decentered in more than one way. As a woman in patriarchal society, she has been traditionally removed from positions of power. She is expected to act out certain roles that do not fulfill her, and which she nevertheless is unable to avoid completely, as the erotic game with Adolfo shows. She is a being created for show, a creation in which the playwright herself participates: she describes Sabina as young and beautiful, her body as lithe and well proportioned, her skin "like that of a green apple; tight" (p. 57). Adolfo, on the other hand, does not have to be handsome to be attractive: he is portrayed as clumsy and likeable (p. 59). Also the sexual encounter between them reveals a certain ambiguity. While it may be interpreted as a liberating experience, Sabina's behavior here points to the difficulty of leaving behind certain feminine roles. Her lack of identity or, in other words, the multiplicity of her identities on stage and in her personal life, bring her close to being a postmodern character as defined by Hutcheon. One can apply Hutcheon's description of the female protagonist in D. M. Thomas' novel *The White Hotel* (1981) to Sabina: "[S]he is presented as the 'read' subject of her own and others' interpretations and inscriptions of her. She is literally the female product of readings" (Hutcheon 161). Although the genre Hutcheon talks about, historical fiction, has little to do with the theatre discussed here, several of Pedrero's characters reveal some of the traits which Hutcheon presents as common in recent postmodern fiction.[7] The metatheatrical aspect of *La noche dividida* expresses the multiplicity of roles Sabina has to perform. As the title indicates, this is a play about split identities, or rather, about a woman's becoming conscious of her split identity, though not yet conscious enough to be aware of the danger of slipping back into one of the predefined feminine roles. "Who am I, really?" she asks Adolfo (p. 61). However, by escaping into Adolfo's arms she avoids the confrontation with Jean Luc and the solitude necessary to find the identity she feels she lacks. While she more or less involuntarily discards Jean Luc, she does not free herself from the patriarchal code that prescribes male company for the traditional female gender role. The play closes when the real confrontation begins. The moment Sabina finds out Jean Luc has been in her apartment, and she realizes she gave away the one chance she had to face him and finally to put her foot down, may be the moment of her worst frustration.

La noche dividida points to the vastness of the problem women writers face in their search for an alternate code. Women's identity in patriarchal society is incomplete—or multiple— because they traditionally have been forced to use a language not their own. Pedrero's theatre is an expression of this dynamic search for identity, an identity which, although necessary, ultimately is not and perhaps should never be something fixed. Pedrero's female characters are discontented. They have taken that step from the unquestioning assumption of a given reality towards a new definition of that reality and ultimately of themselves. Their split identities, their being torn between roles assigned to them by patriarchy and the questioning of these roles, may be one of the reasons for their creativity. Their ability to look beyond the role or roles traditionally assigned to them, the moment of search and uncertainty these characters and their real life models are experiencing, may signal a productive turn away from the single focus and the centered subject. There can never be one central perspective, and the path to emancipation we witness in Pedrero's female characters leads away from the single perspective from which they had been brought up to view society and themselves. Pedrero, in a fashion similar to that of the Argentine playwright Aída Bortnik, does not look for scapegoats. As spectators, we are unable to identify completely with the female protagonists. Their actions often are puzzling (e. g., Ana in *Besos*), and we are likely also to understand and value the other characters' reactions. *La noche dividida* closes with the image of

Jean Luc's disappointment—similar to Camilo's disappointment in *Besos*—when he finds the sleeping couple on the terrace (p. 76).

⳨

A woman's emotional and professional dissatisfaction and her search for a new self-understanding are the focus of *El color de agosto*, first staged in 1988. While the theme is a familiar one in Pedrero's work, here the professional, artistic aspect is treated as more than a mere reflection or extension of the emotional aspect. Although María Dehesa's painting is intimately linked to her emotional development, it is the center of attention in a play that goes beyond the portrayal of a woman's exploration of her inner self by pointing to the creativity such an exploration can generate.

The action evolves around the reunion of two painters who once were very close friends. María Dehesa, the less talented of the two, has become rich and famous, while Laura Antón has stopped painting and now earns her livelihood as a model. The emotionally and at times even physically violent confrontation gradually reveals deep-seated resentment caused by their rivalry with and attraction to each other. María's jealousy of Laura's beauty and talent, and of her love for Juan, led her to break up Laura and Juan's relationship. Heartbroken, Laura left the city, and eventually stopped painting. By losing Laura, however, María lost an important part of her inspiration (p. 45).

Eight years later, María sees Laura's photo in a modeling agency and hires her giving a false name, driven on the one hand by the need to see her again, on the other by the wish to impress and humiliate Laura with her wealth and her fame. After a painful confrontation in which Laura accuses María of being a fake and selling out to commercial interests, and María calls her friend a failure as an artist and human being, the ultimate weapon to destroy female solidarity in patriarchal society is used. In a scene of physical as well as verbal cruelty, María ties Laura to a chair and tells her she married Juan. When Laura surprises her in turn with the disclosure of a letter she received from Juan asking her for a rendezvous, the tension between the two women is resolved anti-climactically. Having lost the battle for Laura's affection and company, María urges her to go and see Juan (p. 53).

Like *La noche dividida*, *El color de agosto* houses the unresolved conflict between the dominant discourse that denies women's independence from men and destroys female solidarity by sanctioning competition for male appreciation, and the subversion of this discourse. The effect the ill-fated love affair with Juan had on Laura, causing her to quit her promising career as artist, may lead us to question the playwright's faith in the possibilities of independent female discourse. However, the need María feels for Laura's friendship, and thus for female solidarity, places the search for a unique female discourse again at the centre of attention. Nevertheless, the disquieting conflict between the male-dominated code and the as yet unassertive female discourse is latent throughout the whole play, manifesting itself openly in the characters themselves.

María Dehesa and Laura Antón are torn by conflicting allegiances. The struggle is obvious in María who, in a desperate attempt to capture Laura's attention, during their childhood continuously subjected herself to her friend's whims. When this failed to have the desired effect, she fell in love with the same man Laura loved, using him as a weapon against her in a very traditional fashion. Their confrontation constantly jumps to and fro between conventional patterns of behavior and rebellion against these patterns. They express violent rivalry and jealousy, founded on the high value women have traditionally placed on their effect on the opposite sex. While Laura tries to ridicule and humiliate María by laughing at her inability to find sexual pleasure, María mocks Laura for not having found a man, and for not having been able to keep Juan interested in her. While on the one hand they use their sexuality against each other, faithful to the gender role assigned to them in patriarchal society, on the other hand their mutual attraction leads them to rebel against this role. They fantasize about a wedding between two women in a unique subversion of the dominant discourse (p. 36–37). When María's involvement in the role-play starts to cross the boundaries between fiction and reality, Laura interrupts the game by asking her if she got married wearing a bridal gown. Juan's invisible presence constantly interrupts the two women's understanding. María urges Laura to forget him (p. 33). Although both are dissatisfied with their relationship with him, they depend on him; María, in order to hurt Laura and thus get her attention, Laura because she still loves him. For María, Juan has lost most of his appeal. Keeping her husband's identity secret, María tells Laura about the gradual death of romantic love. While the partner's clothes strewn about the room and the spilled champagne at first suggest the image of a romantic and bohemian lifestyle, tedium sets in soon, and the champagne will not be allowed to spoil the hardwood floor (p. 39). María knows that her husband is jealous of her success: "Men are not accustomed to be . . . equal to women" (p. 38).

In some ways, Laura is the more honest of the two. She truly loves Juan, and she refuses to sell her art to commercialism (p. 41). On the other hand, she has not painted anything in years, and she is not married to Juan, which is presented as a shortcoming in her life and the root of her personal frustration. María is the perfect product of the consumer society she satisfies with her artwork, an artwork lacking authenticity.

Laura has more talent and perceptiveness than María, as her criticism and suggestions regarding María's paintings indicate, but her creativity is not productive. Both characters have thus failed to pursue an artistic expression true to their inner selves. At the end María takes a first symbolic step towards more authentic self-expression. When Laura leaves the studio, María opens the cage in the womb of a statue of Venus that was serving as model for her last painting, and frees the bird inside. As O'Connor points out, it is significant that the bird, symbol of the creative spirit, is imprisoned in the womb, inside the reproductive system (O'Connor, *Dramaturgas españolas* 48). María's creativity had been stifled not only by her repressed sexuality, but also by her dependence on Laura's inspiration. Laura leaves unwilling to help María, unwilling to pose for her opening the cage in Venus' womb with her hands. Since the Venus has no hands, her mouth will be the tool to free her creativity. The strenuous movement of the Venus, trying to bring her mouth down to unlock the cage, underlines the enormous difficulty of a woman's search for her own voice.

On the quest for independence, the woman and the artist are completely alone. She has to find the tools for her freedom, she has to create her own discourse in a society that is eager to further the pseudo-independence of the commercial artist, but that eyes with suspicion any true and revolutionary deviation from the dominant discourse.

Apart from dealing with the problem of creativity and genuine self-expression, *El color de agosto* explores the difficulties of love relationships, both homosexual and heterosexual. In many ways, Laura and María would be the perfect couple. Their talent and skills complement each other. While Laura may have better ideas and a more vivid imagination, she lacks María's discipline and perseverance. Where Laura is a hopeless romantic, María has a strong practical sense. Their relationship did not last because one felt stifled by the other (p. 30, 45). The fact that they are both women makes things more difficult for them socially, but they realize that, had they been woman and man, their relationship would probably have been just as catastrophic: "Nos destrozaríamos" ["We would tear each other apart"], says María (p. 47).

Love does not provide easy answers in Pedrero's plays: her women protagonists often turn their backs on love relationships, more interested in furthering their own independent development. At the end of *El color de agosto* Laura leaves to see Juan, but the play's central character stays in her studio to set her creative spirit free.

Laura may be interpreted as María's double. Her lack of productivity is reflected by María's lack of creativity. María's final confrontation with her traditional self, in which she chooses love over personal development, leads to a catharsis and a new beginning. Laura and María are the two halves of the female personality, one rooted in tradition, the other stepping towards a more fulfilling role. In Laura's passion and frustration are the seeds of María's freedom.

Frustration, ill-fated love, and self-reflection as the breeding ground for freedom and success are recurring images in several of the plays by the new women dramatists in Spain. *Una comedia de encargo* [A Commissioned Play] (first staged 1988) by Pedrero's contemporary Pilar Pombo explores some of the same themes treated in *El color de agosto*. Victoria is the successful author of commissioned plays that satisfy a mainstream audience with unsophisticated melodrama. Her distress stems both from her unsatisfying job and from her inability to deal with her own sexuality. Victoria has never overcome her love for Marta, a university friend now married and completely absorbed by a materialistic, consumption-oriented society. After a climactic confrontation between Victoria and her friend Esperanza, Victoria realizes she has to change her way of life, to face her own fear and finally to express the things Esperanza accuses her of hiding.

⚮

Many of Pedrero's plays focus on the nature of gender relations and the role love plays in women's search for freedom from traditional roles. While she questions the traditional relationship, several of her plays underline the potentially liberating quality of sexual attraction which can break down social and economic barriers and reconcile the genders separated by the narrow definition of their roles. The short one-act play *Solos esta noche* (1991) uncovers the fear women have of men in a society that is largely based on gender antagonism, and the distrust that isolates different social classes from each other. Two characters alienated from each other by class and gender are forced by circumstances to communicate, and discover that they are both, in their own way, social outcasts. Their sexual encounter becomes an act of subversion against the national capitalist brotherhood.[8]

Carmen, state employee at the Ministry of Culture, and José, unemployed construction worker, are trapped at night in a subway station. The last train seems to have passed, and the gates are locked. The characters have entered a limbo where social mores have no meaning, and anything is possible. Carmen is representative of the contradicitons of the professional woman in an environment still predominantly male. She describes her work place as a collection of "papeles y corbatas" ("papers and ties"). Although she represents the upwardly mobile successful professional, her polished exterior expresses conformity with societal norms. Her identity is shaped by fears and prejudices that keep her trapped in a situation—as discontented wife and professional woman—she has, so far, not dared to transcend. Her initial panic at being alone with José is both an expression of women's fear of men, and the fear the well-to-do have of the working classes. In the course of the play, Carmen overcomes both. Circumstances force her to trust José, whose kindness and vulnerability make her seek intimacy with him. Like Adolfo in *La noche dividida*, José is weak in the eyes of a fast moving, unforgiving society. Injured in a work-related accident, he knows he is considered a loser (p. 80). When Carmen at the end of the play asks José to open his shirt so she can admire his tattoo, and finally has him switch off the flashlight, she lives out a romance novel fantasy—uptown girl meets downtown man—as well as a feminist dream. She breaks out of the role of the frustrated wife, and actively seeks her own pleasure. José's masculinity now attracts rather than threatens her, and their affair—however ephemeral—makes them accomplices against a social order that marginalizes both of them.

Pedrero's women characters explore many different avenues on their search for identity. They play—at times ambiguously—with the social construct of femininity, turning it into a source of strength. As some of Pedrero's plays exemplify, the female characters in the work of the newest women dramatists may not arouse sympathy in the traditional sense, that is, by their kindnesss and/or helplessness. Their search for independence and their wish to assert themselves in a society dominated by the male gender, makes them strong, often scheming and even cruel. If Federico García Lorca's Doña Rosita (*Doña Rosita la soltera* [1935]) or his Adela (*La casa de Bernarda Alba* [1936]) were to reawaken in the plays of a Pedrero or a Resino, they would not wither waiting for a faraway fiancé or hang themselves out of despair and frustration in a society that does not sanction women's self-determination.

❧

Diosdado's and Pedrero's plays reflect the current trends on the Spanish stage regarding not only women playwrights, but the theatrical scene in general.

For Diosdado, the progressive surface seems mainly a bow to the winds of change. Diosdado's "new woman" (Lola in *Anillos de oro*, Alicia in *Olvida los tambores*), and the blandness of her political allegories (*El okapi, Cuplé*), are products of this pseudo-progressiveness which has proven to be so successful commercially. The political themes addressed in a few of her plays do not imply or seek revolutionary change, but are rather a sometimes nostalgic farewell from the old, traditional Spain. While superficially critical of authoritarian leadership and blatant machismo, Diosdado's theatre does not question the deep structure Spain's democratic society has carried over from a long history of sexist political and social organization. On the surface, women are granted independence. They are allowed small rebellions and seemingly important jobs, but ultimately their place is at home, with their husbands and children. Thus, the underlying political message in Diosdado's theatre foregrounds traditional values rather than profound social change, and upholds a separation of the male and the female spheres, and thus the binary male/female opposition itself.

Pedrero's politics are the politics of the intimate. She does not comment on Spanish society and government as a whole, but her plays can be considered as politically more critical than Diosdado's allegories if the term "political" is defined so as to include interpersonal relations among the four walls of the domestic realm. Though Pedrero does not link the private and the public spheres as Bortnik does in her dramatic account of the Argentine experience (e. g. *La historia oficial* [1985]), she is aware of the dangers of constructed gender differences, and in many of her plays questions these by shattering the fixed identities of the female protagonists. Her theatre is a far cry from the unquestioning conservatism of women playwrights under Franco. Ballesteros' *Quiero ver al doctor* (1940), and Suárez de Deza's *Buenas noches* (1952), both of which sanctioned feminine domesticity and devotion to the husband, were in themselves political statements. They supported the *"Kinder, Küche, Kirche"* maxim necessary to help uphold a social structure in which women were not supposed to compete with men in the job market, where no resources were to be spent on women's education, health benefits, and job security. In this sense the work of playwrights like Pedrero, Pombo, Lázaro, or the recent plays by Resino, can be considered political and a challenge to the status quo so resistant to change. These plays breathe fresh air into the Spanish theatrical scene where, nevertheless, the pseudo-progressiveness of a Diosdado or a Reina still gathers most of the attention and the money. Witness to this are the two-year runs of Diosdado's *Los ochenta son nuestros* and of her stoutly conservative *Camino de plata*.

The relatively calm transition from almost four decades of dictatorship to a more or less democratic system generally has not been directly reflected in the work of the women playwrights of the eighties; that is, their theatre is not a political theatre in the way that Kirby has defined it. However, in a wider sense, their theatre has political implications. These dramatists choose to concentrate their attacks on the lingering traces of Franquista society which affect them most directly, on prejudice so deeply entrenched in Spanish society today that it is often overlooked. While sexual freedom and homosexuality up to a certain point— and mostly from a male perspective[9]—have become fashionable, the same cannot be said of feminism. Theatre that offers feminist viewpoints thus can be deemed politically challenging, though in a different way from what we are to witness on the Argentine stage after 1983. In Argentina, some women playwrights consciously link issues of public politics and women's struggle for independence at home, where the dominant male often becomes the symbol for the political oppression outside.

Notes

[1]On the distinction of Female and Feminine, see Toril Moi's article "Feminist, Female, Feminine" in Belsey and Moore, p. 117–132.

[2]Also see Gambaro, "Algunas consideraciones sobre la mujer y la literatura," p. 472–473.

[3]For an interesting approach to Pedrero's theater, based on Hélene Cixous' ideas on the gender of writing, see C. Weiner's article "Gendered Discourse in Paloma Pedrero's *Noches de amor efímero.*"

[4]Resino remarks on this issue in the survey "¿Por qué no estrenan . . . ?" p. 22.

[5]While I could have included the analysis of *Invierno de luna alegre* in this study, the variety of themes addressed in that play dillute the focus on the development of a feminist discourse.   Therefore I chose to discuss the thematically more focussed *La noche dividida*, rather than the award-winning *Invierno.*

[6]*Solos esta noche* was published in 1991 as part of the trilogy *Noches de amor efímero*, which also includes *Esta noche en el parque* and *La noche dividida.*

[7]Hutcheon attempts to define Postmodernism as "a cultural activity that can be discerned in most art forms and many currents of thought today, . . . fundamentally contradictory, resolutely historical, and inescapably political." Postmodernism implies "a critical reworking, never a nostalgic 'return'" of the aesthetic forms and social formations of the past (Hutcheon, *A Poetics of Postmodernism* p. 4).   In the novels Hutcheon discusses, history and identity do not offer a consistent, seemingly objective perspective anymore; the story is not told from the point of view of one centered subject, but from different, often opposing points of view.

[8]Mary Louise Pratt developed the term "national brotherhood" in her article "Women, Literature and National Brotherhood," (Bergmann et al., 1990) basing it on Benedict Anderson's definition of nation as "imagined community" in his book *Imagined Communities: Reflections on the Origin and Spread of Nationalism* (London: Verso, 1983).

[9]See, for example the films directed by Pedro Almodóvar.

Chapter Five

Argentine Theatre:
In Pursuit of Double Militancy

Resistance to dictatorship and the treatment of women's issues are increasingly linked in the most recent work of some of the contemporary Argentine women playwrights, among them Roma Mahieu, Hebe Serebrisky, Nelly Fernández Tiscornia, Gambaro, and Bortnik. This link has become more obvious after the democratic transition (1983), reflecting issues that are far from being resolved in Argentina's young democracy.[1]

The first wavering steps towards democracy were marked by the significant presence of women struggling for freedom from dictatorship. According to Suzana Prates, women played a central role in protesting against the arbitrary use of power by the military junta (10). Elsa de Becerra, of the Mothers of the *Plaza de Mayo*, stresses the role her movement played in organizing the resistance, and in creating a space for the articulation of dissent for militants from proscribed political parties (Fisher 95). Women were also among the victims of the military's infamous *Proceso de reorganización nacional* (Process of National Reorganization). In its report, the CONADEP (National Comission for Disappeared Persons) states that thirty percent of the disappeared in Argentina were women.[2]

A superficial look at the history of women in Argentina may lead the observer to believe there is little or no discrimination based on gender. Sociologist Nora Scott-Kinzer, who in 1967 conducted a study on "Role Conflict of Professional Women in Buenos Aires," was surprised at the active participation of Argentinean women in professional life. Her impressive statistics comparing women professionals in the United States to those in Argentina, are favorable to the latter (50).

Carlson traces the general acceptance and approval of women's education to the second half of the nineteenth century, when Domingo Faustino Sarmiento, a stout defender of women's right to freedom and education, worked to adopt the North American school system in Argentina. By 1910 Argentina was the only country in Latin America, with the exception of Uruguay, "morally and financially committed to the education of women" (83). Fisher points out that in 1989, Argentine women have one of the highest economic participation rates in Latin America (6).

However, gender discrimination was and is deeply rooted in Argentine society. The turn of the century saw the beginnings of Argentine feminism, closely linked to the immigrant movement and to the more affluent sectors of society (hence its failure to appeal to the broad mass of women). While it was mainly a suffrage movement, it contained a strong denunciation of patriarchy. At that time, women were legally classed with unborn children, minors, and the retarded and insane. Wives were denied an identity separate from that of their husbands and needed their permission to enter into legal contracts. Divorce was not possible (Carlson 40). Some of these things have not changed. The loss of independence women experience once they are married—an independence socially acceptable up to a certain point while they are single—is reflected in the low proportion of married women in paid employment in contemporary Argentina (Fisher 6). A woman's place is still the home. The accounts of some of the members of the *Madres* movement speak of a difficult change in their lives when they decided to become public figures (Fisher 42). Without wanting to generalize, Hebe de Bonafini states that, due to the patriarchal social structure, "[m]any women had to fight in secret from their husbands." Work outside the home or, as in the case of the *Madres*, political involvement, did not relieve women from their domestic duties. Laura de Rivelli tells Jo Fisher that, rather than advocating a change in gender-role distribution, women learnt to combine their domestic work with their public activities (97).

According to writer and feminist María Elena Walsh, the military state, Argentina's endemic evil, brainwashed Argentine women with its often repeated slogan *Dios, Patria y Hogar* (God, Fatherland and Hearth). She points out that the repression split the women's movement, by separating women "as group, as class, by age, by service sector"[3] The decade from 1975 to 1985, dedicated internationally to the woman, found little echo in a country ravaged by political terror and intimidation. The collapse of the economy,[4] and a propaganda geared to reinforce women's traditional role worked together to make the struggle for women's rights seem subversive from the point of view of the military state, and irrelevant from the point of view of the resistance. As Feijoó and Jelin point out, the 1976 coup crushed the feminist movement in Argentina. A conference of different women's groups in the *Teatro Municipal General San Martín*, an event associated with the International Year of Women was the last sign of life of feminist groupings before the coup (Feijoó and Jelin 1985: 37).

The large presence of women in the movements toward a democratic transition was not motivated by feminist concerns. Hebe de Bonafini emphasizes this point in an interview with *Alfonsina*, significantly titled "Mis hijos me parieron a mí" ["My children gave birth to me"] by explaining that the Mothers fight for their sons and daughters rather than for themselves in their role as women. In her study of the *Madres de la Plaza de Mayo*, Fisher argues that, from the point of view of the woman who witnesses the economic (and political) misery of her male companion, the vindication of women's rights seems less urgent (5).

In front of the Tribunal of the International Women's Conference in Mexico, in 1974, Domitila Barrios de Chungara underlined the fundamental difference between Betty Friedan-style feminism, and the struggle of the Bolivian miners' wives (Barrios de Chungara 153–54). According to Domitila, an exclusive struggle for women's rights has no justification in a society where men's freedom is not guaranteed.

Argentine women have historically repeatedly stood up for their rights, but their struggle—be it a struggle for women's rights or a struggle of resistance against dictatorship—again and again has been taken out of their hands by seemingly more important or just more powerful social and economic pressures. Argentine governments from Perón in the forties to Alfonsín in the eighties seem to have exploited women voters, ultimately refusing to share power with them. It is in Peronism that we have to seek some of the reasons for the contradictions of the fate of Argentine women and their struggle for participation in politics. After middle- and upper-class feminists like Cecilia Grierson, Alicia Moureau, Elvira Rawson, and Victoria Ocampo had for a long time advocated women's right to vote, Perón granted suffrage to women in 1947, much to the dismay of these stoutly anti-Peronist feminists. Perón and his charismatic wife, Eva, mobilized working class women, recognizing the political power behind this silent majority. Although Eva Perón reassured men of the continued supporting role women were to play after enfranchisement, her rhetoric certainly caused women to be politically more aware and conscious of their power (Carlson 89). According to Martin, Peronist women would play an important role in the struggle against dictatorship between 1955 and 1966 (68).

Argentina's politically unstable course, her wavering between military dictatorship and short-lived civilian governments, seems to be one of the reasons for the heightened political awareness among women. We do not find this to such a degree in Spain, where the military state's arm did not reach into the domestic realm with the brutality of some Latin American dictatorships. In Latin America, the political course forced women to become social protagonists, involved in class struggle, and eventually also in the struggle against *machismo*. Thus the struggle of the *Madres*, who transformed the traditional institution of motherhood into a "mode d'action contre-institutionelle," seemed to pave the way for the emergence of feminist concerns (Martin 82). Their Thursday marches in front of the governmental palace, the *Casa Rosada*, their refusal to be traditional mothers, obliged by convention to resigning themselves to their fate, disconcerted the military and, even today, keeps disrupting the comfortable passivity democracy has meant for too many in Argentina. Through their identity as mothers, wives, or sisters they have conquered a political space that many have used but few have been willing to share. The struggle of the *Madres* and *Abuelas de la Plaza de Mayo* opened the door to overt political dissent, but the parties that joined together in the *Multipartidaria* to call for elections, rejected the participation of the *Madres*.

The young democracy has not changed this outlook. President Alfonsín disapproved of the continuing activities of the Mothers under constitutional government (Fisher 142). This behavior has been in part politically motivated since the fear of upsetting the irascible military is still great. However, it was also Alfonsín who said in an interview with the Spanish magazine *Cambio 16*, about a possible encounter with Margaret Thatcher, that it was difficult to argue with women (Casas 78). The democratic government is subject to the same prejudices and fears as the military dictatorship. The *Madres* continue to be "locas," "crazy" because they keep transgressing the space assigned to them by patriarchy. Such a transgression, though never called feminist by the Mothers, is a feminist statement in itself. The temptation to accept the government's offer of reconciliation with the family members' death, and thus with their murderers, was great, and cost the *Madres* some of their members (Martin 126). However, in Martin's opinion, the movement did not lose its strength during the 1980's.[5]

Hebe Bonafini's criticism of the democratic government, its conciliatory attitude towards the military, and its efforts to appease and render inoffensive the rage of the Mothers with its offers to make heroes out of the disappeared, underlines the political significance of a movement that refuses to be institutionalized.[6] The Mothers reject monuments to the disappeared or the naming of streets to make heroes out of them since this would mean accepting their death (Martin 94).

Feijóo has criticized the *Madres*-movement for their lack of institutionalization and their reliance on emotional appeal, concerned that movements like this one have not questioned women's traditional role ("The Challenge" 88). It seems that this objection stems from a Western middle class style of feminism that poses unrealistic demands on a movement created largely by working class women. It was, after all, the traditional framework under which the Mothers operated and their lack of institutionalization that made them successful spokeswomen for the resistance. And while their goals are, at least not initially, specifically feminist, they assume positions that are among the goals of any feminist movement.[7]

During the dictatorship, the general climate of repression made a struggle exclusively for women's rights seem irrelevant. Playwright Griselda Gambaro has pointed out the primary importance of the fight for survival, a fight that relegated all other struggles to the background (Gambaro, Facio, et al. 45).

Only gradually are politically aware and active Argentine women turning to the advocacy of women's rights, particularly now that the democratic transition has betrayed the hope for a heightened participation of women in the political process. Walsh decries the negligible presence of women in all spheres of government (4). Although 51.03 percent of the voters are women, the political parties present hardly any women candidates. From 1951 to 1983 there has been a steady decrease of women's presence in Congress (from 10 percent to 4.7 percent) (Archenti 128–29). The scant presence of women in politics after 1983 has led writer Aída Bortnik to state in 1987 that, although Argentina came out of a harrowing dictatorship with a large female presence, women appeared to have a larger presence than they really did ("Participar" 59). There is an increasing awareness of the necessity of integrating women into social, economic, and political life, and that the status of Argentine women continues to be undeprivileged in respect to men (Archenti 28). Democratic Argentina has seen the birth of two major journals dealing with feminist issues, *Alfonsina* (1983) and *Feminaria* (1988). Women who had concentrated on the general struggle for political freedom from dictatorship now include women's issues in their protest about the wavering course of the newly established democracy. Several of the *Madres* state their interest in equal rights for women, while still rejecting the term "feminist" (Fisher 158).

This heightened awareness extends also to Argentine women playwrights, who in some cases have developed from the initial denial of the existence of gender discrimination to its acknowledgement and criticism. While Bortnik denies having experienced male prejudice during her university studies and as a writer, her plays and filmscripts mirror, next to her concern about

Argentina's political development, an increasing awareness of gender inequality ("Participar" 58). In an interview conducted in 1978, Gambaro denied the existence of discrimination against the woman writer. She claimed any discrimination was class- rather than gender-based (Interview with Garfield 68, 70). Six years later she says that the women characters in her more recent work have become "more dynamic, more active." She attributes this to a heightened consciousness on her part of what it means to be a woman (Interview with Betsko, Koenig 194).

The "leaden years" of the *Proceso* mobilized women politically. The methods of repression and propaganda the military employed to enforce their economic program reached into the heart of the poorer sectors of Argentine society. The government-controlled media urged parents to denounce their children if they suspected them of belonging to guerrilla movements (Fisher 26). The destruction of the family unit by illegal detentions and disappearances brought women out onto the streets, believing themselves to be stronger than men, to "have more willpower" (Bonafini, qtd. in Fisher 60). The comments of writers, playwrights, and artists, fragmented by censorship, self-censorship and exile, nevertheless, continued to be one of the last refuges of a very restricted freedom of expression. While the media were under the almost complete control of the government, theatre, probably considered too elitist to be dangerous, continued to survive as long as it used a language unintelligible to the general audience. Ordaz comments that the language used after 1976, is "cryptic" and "oblique" (Fernández "1949–1983" 150).

In contrast to Spain under the Franco regime, Argentina had several very active, highly political women playwrights. Although they used—and frequently still use—a language traditionally male-dominated and often wrote from a male point of view, their social and political commitment differentiates them from their Spanish colleagues. Comparing North American and Latin American women poets, Gambaro points out the different angles from which these two groups view the situation of women. In Latin America, gender-related issues have not received the same critical attention given to political concerns,

72

even by women writers themselves ("Algunas consideraciones" 471–72). This applies to many of the Argentine woman playwrights who, like Roma Mahieu, Bortnik, and Gambaro, have frequently assigned their female characters traditional roles, while their message is one of utter discontent with the political establishment.

Contrary to Spanish women playwrights under the dictatorship, the Argentines profess overt political commitment. Gambaro goes as far as saying that all Argentine theatre "is more or less political " The political point of view, rather than a goal, is "a necessity" (Interview with Betsko, Koenig 186).

A decade of a very unstable democracy is not a sufficiently long time span to judge accurately any recent development in the work of the women dramatists. It seems, however, as if the skepticism with which several of them view the transition has not yet allowed them to turn to more personal themes. So far, the search for individual fulfillment, the development of an identity outside traditionally assigned gender roles, the crisis of the male-female relationship, have only seldom surfaced as themes independent from the preoccupation with Argentina's political future. The explosion of cheap commercialism, the "destape visual y lingüístico" that accompanied the transition just as it did in Spain, cannot hide the concern about the dangers facing democracy (Cosentino 157).

Amid and despite the profusion of critical voices that echo the reactions of Spanish critics from a few years ago, new plays are being written, often revisionist in character and skeptical concerning Argentina's fate. Among the most significant are Gambaro's *Del sol naciente* (1983), Eduardo Pavlovsky's *Potestad* (1985), Bortnik's *Primaveras* (1985), Nelly Fernández Tiscornia's *Made in Lanús* (1986), and Osvaldo Dragún's *Arriba, corazón* (1987).

The next two chapters focus on the work of two women playwrights, both among the best-known contemporary Argentine writers. Bortnik and Gambaro are highly political dramatists who were forced to flee the repression in their country. They returned to Argentina during the dictatorship to continue their analysis of dictatorial society from within. The study of their work from the early seventies up to 1988 looks at the political content and the changes in their perception of traditional gender roles. We will see that, while the political commitment of these playwrights has unwaveringly continued, regardless of the political changes Argentina has undergone, a new perspective has developed in their work. They seem to have become gradually more aware of women's issues as a relevant field of political engagement, even though this awareness does not yet reach the comparatively strong tones of a Paloma Pedrero or a Pilar Pombo. Bortnik's and Gambaro's rebellious heroines, whose struggle is first political, and only secondly a struggle for women's rights, may be seen as a reflection of the significant presence of women at the crucial moments of Argentina's transition to democracy.

Notes

[1] Crucial events defining the democratic transition in Argentina are Argentina's defeat in the Falklands (Malvinas) in 1982, and the democratic elections in 1983.

[2] Gambaro, Facio, et al. *El Periodista* 33, 26 April 1985, p. 45.

[3] Interview with Walsh in *Alfonsina* 1 (Dec. 1983), p. 5, 7.

[4] Rock writes that "the near 50 percent plunge in real wages in 1976 was the fastest and steepest ever" (p. 368).

[5] "[C]ontrairement aux partis politiques, qui changent leurs consignes en laissant tomber aujourd'hui ce qu'ils avaient celebré hier, les MPM [Mères de la Plaçe de Mai] ont non seulement maintenu les consignes initiales, mais les ont élargies." (Martin, p. 126).

[6] See Bonafini, "No vamos a claudicar."

[7] The Mothers have been sought out by numerous European Feminist organizations. When they were interviewed by *Cahiers du Feminisme* in 1981, they base their success on their lack of internal organization: "Nous n'avons pas de structure interne [. . .] Notre specificité est de ne pas être structurées, et c'est pour celà que nous sommes aussi nombreuses." (qtd. in Martin, p. 115–116).

Chapter Six

Aída Bortnik:
Between Femininity and Feminism

The five-year-old Gaby, sitting in a rocking chair in the final scene of *La historia oficial*, waiting for parents who will never return for her, is one of the most compelling images in recent Argentine film history. Gaby's song, which is also the theme song of this movie co-authored by Bortnik and Luis Puenzo, contains strong references to the Argentina of military dictatorship. Argentina is "el país del no me acuerdo," a country where people choose to forget rather than assume responsibility, where every step is uncertain and often a step backwards (p. 134).

The story of Gaby, child of *desaparecidos*, is probably the most damning accusation found in Bortnik's work of the more or less open complicity of Argentina's upper middle class with the military regime. However, Bortnik's plays and scripts are pervaded by a sense of the social and political responsibility of the writer (Interview, *Primaveras* 20). Like Gambaro, she condemns the noncommital writer or intellectual whose supposed innocence or naïveté she calls "repugnant".

From her first play, *Soldados y soldaditos* (1972), to the revisionist *Primaveras* [Springs] (1985), Bortnik has confronted and analyzed Argentine reality, looking for its evils mostly within the four walls of the domestic realm. She largely blames individual laziness and lack of courage for the flawed course of Argentine politics and the harrowing consequences of military dictatorship in her country. Much as does Gambaro, she places the responsibility on everybody's personal conduct. Bortnik's work often reflects a disillusionment about the loss of a golden era where those ideals were still intact, similar to the disappointment felt by some in the United States about the loss of the spirit of the sixties. Sometimes these ideals are embodied in a quasi-mythical father-figure (*Papá querido*) [Dear Father]; at other times they are placed somewhere in the Republican trenches in Spanish Civil

War (*Primaveras*). Her work seeks to restore overused words like Honor, Dignity, Solidarity and Justice to their original meaning (Interview, *Primaveras* 13).

Bortnik's plays and screenplays follow a fairly steady course of increased political directness which seems to run parallel to the decreasing rigor of censorship in theatre and film towards the end of the *Proceso* years. *Soldados y soldaditos* (1972), a show written for café-concert, is described by Bortnik as the pacifist analysis of the military profession throughout history. *Soldados* had some problems with censorship under the regime of General Lanusse, but was nevertheless highly successful in Buenos Aires and on its tour around the nation (Interview, *Primaveras* 11). From 1976 on, Bortnik was continually censored. She went into exile in Spain from 1976 to 1979, when she returned to work on the screen play for *La isla*. Her uncompromising views brought her a large number of death threats even during the last months of the *Proceso* regime, in 1983 (Avellaneda *Censura* II: 247). *Primaveras*, a play she started in 1980 about the destruction of every political "spring" in Argentine politics, was not to be staged until after 1983 (Interview 12).

After the political changes in 1983, she warned against superficial optimism, pointing to the instability of Argentina's political course, and reminding her fellow Argentines of the high price they had to pay in advance for a fragile democracy (Interview 19).

The coherence of Bortnik's discourse regarding her view of Argentine politics is not quite as present when she addresses women's issues. Like Gambaro, Bortnik links the macro-political and the micro-political in her development of a feminist discourse. In contrast to Gambaro, though, who has women transcend the limitations of their traditional role by making them passionate and active critics of authoritarian rule, Bortnik's female characters often withdraw to more passive domestic roles.

Bortnik distinguishes between two completely opposed, gender-specific ways of seeing. Similar to Diosdado's work, Bortnik's theatre identifies the male perspective as public, active, and idealistic, and male discourse as highly ideological. Women, on the other hand, form the quiet epicenter around which the (male) world circles frantically, and perhaps hopelessly. They hold the key to the truth underlying all matter, a truth which survives the political and social changes. This distinction— patterned after Yin and Yang, the two opposing principles in ancient Chinese philosophy—breaks down to some degree when Bortnik leaves the symbolic-allegorical realm typical of most of her work. While Bortnik is certainly concerned with a critique of gender discrimination, and attempts to overcome the latter by underlining the meaningfulness and importance of the values traditionally associated with women, in most of her work women remain defined and confined by predetermined roles. The line between description and prescription in her portrayal of women as peaceful mediators and nurturers is thin.

Bortnik's plays to a certain extent reflect what she said in "Participar desde lo propio." She denies the existence of gender discrimination in Argentine society, citing her own experience as an example, but at the same time she points out the absence of women from the political process. She criticizes certain flaws in male-female relations but rarely questions role distribution itself. Women's role is essentially to care for their men and help them fulfill their ideals. Bortnik expects them, furthermore, to have a political voice, somehow overlooking the inherent contradiction between their domestic position of inequality and their expected participation in politics. Curiously enough, it is in *La historia oficial*, a script written together with a male colleague, where a woman is shown to become politically aware and emotionally independent from her husband when her worldview is questioned in the light of recent political events. A plot particularly sensitive to feminist concerns reveals that a fulfilled life as mother and professional does not yet create an independent woman, and that an emotional reaction to a distressing social and political reality is not enough. "Crying does not help at all," Sara tells Alicia in *La historia oficial* (p. 121). This call to action and participation, directed to women in a society where men have failed, is nowhere as present in Bortnik's work as in this script, which, nevertheless, also suffers some of the pitfalls of a discourse shaped by patriarchy. Although men fail and experience deep frustration in most of the plays discussed here, women's role generally does not exceed the responsibility for helping men along on their quest for self-fulfillment. However, the unhappiness women consistently feel in Bortnik's work is a certain sign of dissatisfaction and offers a starting point for a feminist reading of her work.

⚜

In 1981 Bortnik defined *Papá querido* as the ideological and aesthetic synthesis of everything she had written until then (Introduction to *Papá querido* 25). This proves to be true even in 1984, when *Primaveras* takes up the same theme of the frustration of ideals we find in a very condensed form in *Papá querido*. Since this play itself contains no overt reference to the Argentine context, its political meaning within this context unfolds mostly within the framework of *Teatro Abierto*. *Teatro Abierto* was a theatrical event that brought together playwrights, directors, and actors in an effort to revitalize the Argentine scene (Población "La Compañía" 48). Pross observes that *Teatro Abierto* 1981, the first and tremendously successful in a series of festivals, came at a moment of apparent cultural stagnation, due to the peremptory control the government exercized over all creative venues (Pross 84). The enthusiasm of all participants and the extremely low ticket prices evoked an audience response that contradicted any assertions that theatre is dead or dying in contemporary society. The as yet unexplained fire that destroyed the *Teatro del Picadero* where the event was scheduled to take place made the goal of exercising freedom of expression even more urgent. Among the objectives pursued were also the exploration of new forms of production as a reaction against commercialism, the awakening of the public's interest in theatre, and the bringing together of everybody in the Thespian family for the creation of new ideas and a feeling of solidarity. The focus of the 1981 festival was more on political content than aesthetics, a focus that was to shift later on.

In *Papá querido*, Electra, Carlos, Clara, and José meet for the
first time in the house of their father, who has recently committed
suicide. He had them summoned there after his death to receive
his legacy. The powerful presence of the father, notwithstanding
his absence from the stage, converts him into a figure of almost
mythical dimensions. Allusions to his vagabond life, his travels,
his fantastic promiscuity, and the fact that his children had never
met each other before, reinforce this impression. Of the four, only
Clara remembers having been held by him (p. 29). The only
contact they had with their father was through the letters he
wrote to them regularly.

The memory of the father calls forth very different reactions
from his four children, reactions that range from love and
admiration to anger and resentment. The strongest characters
and antagonists in the play are the absent father and Carlos.
Carlos, a forty-five-year old doctor disillusioned with his life, is
angry at his father and what he perceives as a life-long tyranny.
The play gradually reveals that his anger is rooted in his inability
to live up to his father's—and maybe his own—expectations. He
is bitter about the control his father always exerted in his life, both
through his letters, and through his gifts. The father's letters are
the central motif in *Papá querido*. While Clara cherished them,
Carlos had stopped answering them years before, when he had
begun feeling guilty about his failure to live up to his father's
expectations (p. 35).

Both Clara's and Carlos' reactions are justified in the play. In
the character of Electra, whose name alludes to her close
relationship with her father, the contrasting feelings of the other
siblings are held in balance. While she seems to share some of
Carlos' frustration, she also understands her father's failure and,
thus, his humanity. She suspects that her father became aware of
the emptiness of his own dreams, when he realized his inability
to put them into practice. She believes that he wanted to warn
them against similar failure by gathering them and returning the
letters they had written to him in the course of their lives.

The loss of ideals is something experienced by all characters
with the exception of Clara. She continues to see only the love
her father felt for her. Rather than the act of aggression Carlos

sees in the return of the letters, Clara perceives this as an expression of his affection (p. 38).

Electra combines the emotional reactions of the other characters in a rational way. In her, those reactions find their justification and are, at the same time, channeled towards a moral lesson. Electra loved her father as Clara and the people in the town did, but she also perceives his shortcomings and seems determined to learn from his failure. The bittersweet ending of the play underscores the difficulty of this task. When the four characters recite a letter to their "querido papá" in which they promise to become the perfect human beings their father had expected them to to be, the difficulty of fulfilling such expectations is obvious (p. 38).

The play delivers both a praise of the great values of Freedom, Solidarity, Dignity, Justice, and Love, and a warning against underestimating the difficulty of putting them into practice. Bortnik seems to be preoccupied with two issues in this and in subsequent plays. On the one hand, she is concerned with the importance of individual conduct and its reflection on society as a whole. Clara's loving and accepting simple-mindedness here is more helpful than Carlos' aggressive behavior. However, the frustration Carlos feels points to Bortnik's other central concern: the blindness toward the complexity of human feelings and emotions to which the pursuit of lofty ideals may lead. Carlos' criticism is justified in that his father did not regard his children so much as human beings but as pawns for his own idealistic scheming. He manipulated them by giving them names with revolutionary meanings: Carlos is *Germinal*, Jose is *Ateo*. He forgot that both he and his children were only human. While always stressing the importance of Freedom and Justice, Bortnik criticizes the intolerance of the relentless revolutionary. In her interview with Morero, she regrets the bloodshed caused by the "dirty war" of the mid-seventies in Argentina, when, on both sides of the political spectrum, some thought that their terrorist actions would create a society more just. She rejects the arrogance of those individuals and movements that claim a providential role for themselves (Interview 17). While Bortnik leaves no doubt that she sympathizes with the ideas of the father in *Papá querido*, she also emphasizes that the teaching of revolution, without an awareness that human beings are more than just tools, is wrong and ultimately leads to failure.

In a country plagued by the excesses of a military dictatorship, this play, with its reference to the loss of revolutionary ideals and the incendiary rhetoric of the letter to the father at the end, must have had quite a strong impact. This impact, however, is lost when the play is taken out of its context. In fact, the inflammatory rhetoric of the letter seems to acquire an ironic tinge which can lead to a completely different reading of the play, making it much more skeptical and pessimistic than Bortnik may have intended. One might argue that it is in this ambiguity that the true interest of *Papá querido* lies.

The play establishes the binary opposition between male and female that feminist theorists like Kristeva and Moi strive to deconstruct.[1] Clara combines all the characteristics of femininity Moi defines as a social construct women in patriarchy are supposed to accept as natural (Moi 123). She loves and accepts without judging or questioning. She remembers her father's gestures of affection rather than debate the meaning of his revolutionary rhetoric. Carlos, on the other hand, is aggressive, skeptical, unyielding. He understands the reasons for his frustration, and seeks to blame someone else for his failure (p. 35).

Electra empathizes with both positions, but sees farther than her siblings. While Electra has this deeper understanding, it is the men's task to fight it out among themselves. José reminds Electra of his responsibility, as male, to defend the opposite gender, and asks her nor to interfere in the brothers' argument (p. 37). For the feminist critic, this may well throw a dubious light on the figure of the father, who left behind cultural baggage that—paradoxically but not surprisingly—combined political idealism with conventional gender roles.

The father figure combines many of the traits traditionally associated with the male gender. The protagonists repeatedly refer to his promiscuity, his adventurism, and to his great intellectual capacity. Despite his short-comings, he was a leader and role model for his children and the people in his town. In keeping with what he taught José about his duty to defend women, he gave his children names indicative of their distinct gender roles. While Carlos and José are *Germinal* and *Ateo*, names associated with creativity and the questioning of authority, *Electra* alludes to attachment to the father. *Minerva*, name of the Roman goddess of Wisdom, is a very significant name for Clara. Clara's wisdom is not the debating, questioning intelligence of Carlos, but the wisdom that lies in the tranquility of the person in harmony with herself. The secret of this wisdom is the capacity to love unquestioningly and to display the least possible resistance to the hardships of life. As in the case of Diosdado's work, Ellmann's definition of female idiocy versus male lunacy comes to mind.[2] While Ellmann underlines the negative meaning of the feminine stereotype, Bortnik charges it with a positive content. The "supposed incapacity of women for impersonal thought" that Ellman describes as one of the fundamental gender differences established by patriarchy, in Bortnik becomes the personal sense the male characters lack. This sense, together with the intuitive capacity, another feminine trait identified by Ellmann (112), may make them, according to the playwright, more fit to survive than their male partners, and more capable to shape a society truly democratic.

∂ℚ

Bortnik finished her play *Domesticados* around the same time she staged *Papá querido*. Again, the central theme is the loss of youthful revolutionary ideals and, as the title indicates, the "taming" of the protagonists by passive, deadening domesticity.

The plot unfolds around the break-up of the marriage of Ana and Julio. Julio leaves Ana and their son, Lito, to pursue his affair with Ana's best friend, Alejandra. Alejandra is the independent, "untamed" woman Ana once used to be, and Julio mistakenly believes she can save him from his own frustration. Meanwhile, Ana tries to rebuild her life alone with Lito. Shocked by her loss of identity and the lack of direction in her life, she unsuccessfully tries to be independent. When Julio in the end returns, it is very doubtful whether they will be able to resume their life together in a meaningful way.

As in *Papá querido* and later in *Primaveras*, Bortnik here voices her concern about the ease with which idealistic individuals are coopted into a materialistic, self-centered way of life. While the tale of Ana and Julio is the universal one of frustrated marriage, in the Argentine context it contains a strong accusation against the position of the disinterested spectator. Although the protagonists realize they have strayed from the path they chose when they were newly married, there seems to be little they can do about it now. Julio's list of things he wants to do with Alejandra is nothing more than a rebellion in a fishbowl. His dreams of jungles and wild tigers, of life in the countryside, mountain climbing, and nude bathing in the ocean are the result of a frustration from which Alejandra refuses to save him. She belittles his dreams, recognizing them as symptoms of a very vulgar midlife crisis, to which he seeks a very vulgar solution: she is to provide him all that adventure, "almost without leaving [the] bed" (p. 21).

Like Julio, Ana needs other people's help to stand on her own feet. At first she does not realize that the friends on whom she wants to rely have to deal with their own frustrations—like Quique with his homosexuality—, or are not reliable anymore— like Alejandra, her best friend and now "la otra." Both Ana and Julio are responsible for the deterioration of their relationship. As in most of her work, Bortnik is very careful not to portray any of the characters as scapegoat. The audience's identification with Ana against Alejandra is turned around in the final scene, when the two friends and rivals come face to face for the first and only time in the play. Here, Alejandra's accusations reveal Ana's self-righteous and insensitive side that had prompted Alejandra to seek revenge when she started her affair with Julio. She places some of the responsibility for the failure of the marriage with Ana herself, and blames her for having encouraged his dependency on her (Ana) (p. 63).

Although the reasons for the protagonists' frustration are never explained in detail, the roots for it are to be sought in the loss of their youthful political idealism. Julio equates his withdrawal from political activism with a loss of masculinity. Although he still believes in the same things he believed in when he was seventeen, now he does not "have the balls" to say them out loud (p. 64). Ana shares his frustration. She feels that instead of changing the world, only they changed, coopted by the daily routine of family and profession.

The marital problems of Julio and Ana in *Domesticados* are treated from what initially seems a thoroughly feminist perspective. Ana's determination to continue her life as usual after Julio has left the house is questioned by her son, Lito, who reminds her that everything she had ever done, had been done for her husband (p. 11). With independence forced upon her, Ana re-evaluates her previous role as housewife and mother. She compares her fate to that of a disposable doll that, with the help of a little key, performs all the duties of the homemaker and the faithful wife (p. 52). However, the honesty of this feminist critique is put into question by Ana's subsequent behavior, which makes it difficult to read *Domesticados* as a feminist play. Ana's efforts go no further than the superficial transformation of her appearance. She cuts her hair—Julio had preferred it long—and starts an exercise class. When she tries to convince José, director of the school where she teaches, to give her more teaching hours, she uses all her feminine charm, attempting to be "sophisticated and seductive" (p. 31). José's response uncovers serious flaws in Ana's character, who in the past had obviously enjoyed enticing José's desire, while she at the same time had rejected his advances. Ana uses José to make Julio jealous, kissing him in front of her husband. Her (deserved?) punishment comes when that night José refuses to leave her apartment, and tries to rape her. Here Bortnik seems to have gone from a feminist description of a failed marriage to an anti-feminist justification of male violence: she "asked for it." José is paradoxically portrayed as the tortured victim of Ana's machinations, since his love for her makes him defenseless (p. 58). Although José's condescending behavior toward Ana's homosexual cousin casts a dubious light on his ethical integrity, the audience is forced to understand his suffering and, together with the protagonist herself, recognize

Ana's guilt. The scene ends with both of them entering Ana's bedroom, linked in a tight embrace.

On first look, Alejandra seems to embody the feminist ideal of the independent woman. She has control of her life, and refuses to relinquish it, shattering Julio's hope for a permanent relationship with her. As a girl, she was already strong and combative. According to Quique, her aggressiveness is the reason she never found a husband (p. 24). If Alejandra's personality leads us to believe in her independence and in the strength of her personal choices, we learn toward the end of the play that remaining single was not a conscious personal decision, but one that grew out of suffering. Ana had destroyed Alejandra's great love by making her look like a fool in front of him, and arousing his interest in herself (p. 60–61). Alejandra's affair with Julio was thus motivated by the desire of revenge.

While *Domesticados* starts out questioning traditional gender roles and analyzing a woman's identity crisis when she is all of a sudden stripped of her role as loving housewife, the play ultimately endorses traditional role-models. While men outwardly seem to be in control of their lives, the female protagonists in this play use and manipulate them. While men act out of love, idealism, and search of (spiritual and intellectual) redemption, women's actions here are motivated by revenge, hate, or simply to achieve security and financial gain.

When Ana and Julio embrace in the final scene, and the alarm clock José forgot under the pillow starts to ring, it becomes clear that there is no room for comfort left, neither between them nor in their own conscience.

Like *Papá querido*, *Domesticados* leaves it up to the reader or viewer to trace parallels between the characters' frustrations and Argentina's political fate. The theme and even several of the characters are essentially the same as in *Primaveras* and *La historia oficial*, the two works discussed here that were published or released after 1983. While in *Domesticados* the references to political unrest are relatively vague, and in *Papá querido* politics are confined to mere rhetoric, the next two works under discussion deal with concrete political events. Both *Primaveras* and *La historia oficial* state that there is not and should not be any distinction or separation between the private and the public realms. And yet, that distinction remains largely in place when Bortnik addresses gender issues.

⚭

Primaveras, a play Bortnik was able to finish writing only in 1983, was first staged in 1984 at the Teatro Municipal General San Martín. Although the lessening of censorship in democratic Argentina made it possible for her to name certain important dates in her country's history, and even to include a reference to the "disappeared" under the *Proceso*, she still relies mainly on the portrayal of human relationships (Interview 14).

Primaveras looks at the development of the personal lives of three couples, who are friends, against the background of three crucial dates in Argentine history: 1958, 1973, and 1983. Each of these dates stands for a political opening, the quick frustration of which, leads the protagonists and the audience to increased skepticism at the arrival of each new democratic spring. In 1958, the military regime of General Pedro E. Aramburu was replaced by the civilian government of Arturo Frondizi. In 1973 the Peronist candidate Héctor Cámpora—essentially a temporary stand-in for Perón—followed General Alejandro Lanusse's regime. His government aroused hopes that were quickly and thoroughly dispelled under Perón's short, ill-fated rule and the brutal repression of civil unrest under Isabel Perón, who assumed the presidency following her husband's death in 1974. 1983 witnesses the last turn of the tide viewed with increased skepticism and even pessimism by Bortnik. The play gives some room for hope that this spring will be followed by a summer but, as one protagonist says: "Don't talk to me about the summer . . . There are centuries left until the summer!" (p. 96).

The personal hopes and frustrations of the characters mirror these events to a degree where the personal and the historical become indistinguishable. The play weaves together the personal and the political in a tripartite composition. Each of the three *cuadros* is structured around a family celebration that takes place against the background of a change in the political climate of the country. In the first *cuadro* or act, we witness José and Delia's wedding celebration which, like the other two festivities, takes place on the farm the three couples have just bought. In the second act, the same friends and relatives celebrate Angélica's daughter's fifteenth birthday. Angélica is José's sister, and married to the materialistic Roberto. The third act deals with Delia and José's twenty-five-year wedding anniversary. From the first act on, the happiness and high expectations for the future already carry the seeds of despair. Bernardo, José's father, is unhappy with the wedding (p. 36). Sergio's mad love for his wife Lucía forebodes evil, and Roberto's materialism clashes with Enrique's revolutionary convictions (p. 42).

In the first act the symbolic subplot also starts, prompting director Beatriz Mátar to describe the play as inscribed in magic realism (Interview 25). The four basic symbolic elements are the farm on the edge of civilization, the tree Bernardo and his wife Natalia plant at the beginning of the play, a flute that is heard at different moments throughout the play, and the tiger that escapes from a nearby circus at the end of Act One. Related symbols are the horse Angélica wishes to have at the beginning of the first act, and whose death is revealed towards the end of the play, and the wind which symbolizes unrest and change. The different symbols are associated with different characters in the play. The tree, which stands for hope and stability, is linked to Natalia, whose idea it was to plant the tree, her mother, Clara, and her daughter-in-law, Delia. Clara, the grandmother whose love for life is unchanged throughout the play, climbs into the tree at the end of Act Two to get a different view of the world. She recommends that her great-granddaughter's boyfriend, a hot-headed young revolutionary, get a view from the top of a tree, thus gaining the perspective he lacks (p. 85). At the end of the play Delia plants another small tree. The words of encouragement she speaks to it sum up what in *Primaveras* comes to be the female, or, rather, feminine worldview. She suggests that in bringing up their son, her husband forgot the things that really matter in life since he was more concerned with teaching him lofty ideals and political rhetoric. The small tree represents a future where these "private" values, like love and caring, are cherished again.

The flute is a symbol closely linked to the tree. When Delia discovers the tree José's parents planted at the end of the first act, the flute is heard (p. 47). As the play progresses, the flute sounds louder and the melody becomes more sophisticated. The growing tree and the flute are symbols of hope and of a more profound understanding of reality that looks beyond the stormy seas of the loud political changes. Like the tree, the flute is a symbol associated with some of the women in the play: only Natalia, Delia's daughter Paula, Delia herself, and Clara can hear it. At the beginning of the third act, when everybody is getting ready for the anniversary celebration, Paula hears the flute and calls her brother. Unable to hear it, he directs his attention to the wind, encouraging it to blow stronger (p. 88).

The wind that appears in Delia's nightmares and makes her scream forebodes unrest and change, and is associated with some of the male characters. For Alejandro it means hope while Delia fears it (p. 68). While the tree and the flute promise a stability and a happiness that is more a hopeful projection of the future than a reality in the play, the wind and the roaming tiger symbolize the unrest that is necessary if change is to come about, but that is not enough to make it successful. José and Enrique are crucial figures in this respect. José, the poet, identifies with the tiger that breaks loose at the end of the first act. He feels that, like the tiger, he needs wide spaces to roam, and blames his marriage for his lack of freedom (p. 60). His romantic attraction to Sergio's wife, the beautiful Lucía, acts as a substitute for the dreams he himself has never put into practice. Like Julio in *Domesticados*, he feels the need to recuperate the lost idealism of his youth with forbidden love, all the while blind to his own personal failure.

Enrique, José's unmarried friend, embodies the freedom of which everybody else is a little envious. In 1958 he preaches revolution to his friends and proposes a toast to the future and to the revolution (p. 42). He is absent in the second act, possibly in exile. In the third act he reappears to remind his friends of the bet he proposed during Delia's and José's wedding celebration, when he wanted everyone to bet on her or his own future (p. 53). Although only Delia ever spoke aloud her promise for the future, they all know that they failed to realize their own dreams. Like his father, José feels he has taught his children ideals that sound false in his own crumbling world. Angélica lives a completely frustrated family life. Her daughter, Viviana, lives abroad and has hardly any contact with her parents, and her husband Roberto has proved to be the egotistical, greedy person Enrique has always known him to be (p. 93). Like José, Angélica puts the disenchantment they all feel, in political terms: the ideals of 1968 have been betrayed. Mementos from the years of student protest, have lost their socio-political relevance, and are buried in museums (p. 97).

Although Bortnik here links the abandonment of political activism and the deterioration of ideals among the members of her own generation to the disenchantment felt in other Western countries like France and Spain, the political events she refers to are Argentine. As Enrique points out, Angélica attends "el acto de la Plaza," that is, the Thursday demonstrations of the Mothers of the Disappeared. Viviana's young boyfriend who caused havoc with his revolutionary rhetoric during the second act, is now dead. Clara's astonishment about the young man's death mirrors Bortnik's comment on the cruel times of the *Proceso*, when being young equalled being suspect (Interview 15).

As in *Papá querido*, Bortnik takes great care in underlining the importance of compromise between conflicting political factions. The *joven* is portrayed as too hot-headed and intolerant. Climbing Clara's tree would enhance and broaden his perspective. José, the protagonist torn between the wild tiger inside him and what Bortnik conceives of as a deeper understanding of reality, voices Bortnik's concerns in Act Two, namely that one should refrain from seeing things in black and white, and that being able to listen to the other side is essential for a future understanding (p. 70). Although the revolutionary Enrique is the catalyst of the final confrontation between the characters and their own wasted lives, Bortnik leaves no doubt as to Enrique's own incompleteness. Like the father in *Papá querido*, he has forgotten the needs of the individual over his concern for a vaguely defined "humanidad" (p. 100).

José and Delia, the central characters in the play, embody the attitudes on which, according to Bortnik, a better future may be built. Delia's generosity and self-sacrifice—she quietly accepts the knowledge of José's attraction to Lucía—, and José's understanding of his own shortcomings make a new beginning possible.

The farm on the edge of civilization, close to the unknown, uncultivated land where everything is still possible, becomes the central symbol for Argentina's uncertain future. Natalia's warning against the difficulty of creating something new in the inhospitable environment contains a lesson the young idealists of the first act have yet to learn (p. 47).

Primaveras portrays a world in which male political rhetoric has failed. The play proposes, in somewhat vague terms, a political practice that is based on traditionally masculine *and* feminine values. Clara's and Delia's quiet wisdom and nurturing qualities are viewed as essential for a more meaningful and successful "Spring." However, the fact that the symbolic plot in this play is structured around a fundamental opposition between male and female, may be problematic from a feminist viewpoint. The tree and the flute, symbols of quiet strength and faith in the future, are associated with female characters, while the roaming, restless tiger and the wind are associated with male characters. Clara, her daughter Natalia, and the latter's daughter-in-law, Delia, are nurturing, loving, mediating beings concerned with the happiness of others. Delia's purpose in life is to love selflessly. She is the only one to bet openly on her future when Enrique suggests the bet in the first act. This bet is concerned exclusively with her future children, and with José's success. When Enrique reminds her that she should bet on her own future, she replies that she is doing just that when she bets on her husband's. All she wishes for herself is to be able to love others even better (p. 58). While José fails as a poet and feels disillusioned with life and the world around him, Delia keeps her promise. Like Clara and Natalia, she firmly believes everything will eventually turn out well, something that cannot be said of the male protagonist.

Throughout the whole play, José questions his decisions and lucubrates about his frustration. José and Delia's marriage closely resembles the marriage of José's parents, Bernardo and Natalia. Bernardo is a skeptical, never-content character whose high expectations of life and of his children have been disappointed. Natalia, on the other hand, has great faith in life and in love (p. 44).

Bortnik's binary opposition of female versus male plays into the hands of the discourse that establishes this dichotomy in the first place. While she advocates a society more just, where Freedom and Solidarity are more than over-used rhetoric, she seems to believe that such a society can be created on the foundation of a male/female dichotomy. According to Kristeva, the opposition of man/woman belongs to metaphysics. She questions the usefulness of sexual identity at a time in which, according to her, the concept of identity itself is being questioned (214–15). Bortnik, however, does not conceive of the opposition of male/female as rivalry, but rather as a productive balance. In the description of her characters she foregrounds their gender-specific identity. Hers is a world where the subject is still intact, but where next to the legitimate male voice emerges the legitimate female speaker, both, however, inscribed in separate spheres.

As in Diosdado's plays, political talk and action are depicted as male domain. When Viviana calls her father "ideologically confused," her boyfriend bursts into laughter and calls her a little baby. He tells her how beautiful and sweet she is, to which Viviana responds: "You are beautiful too when you are not talking about politics" (83–84). Once again, the world of women is not the public world of politics. Their language is the language of love; their realm, the private realm of intimate family relations.

Angélica, the only politically committed woman in the play, is unhappily married, this fact having greater weight than her politically-rooted frustration. Also very interesting is that more importance is attached to her having disappointed her father, Bernardo, than to her own disillusionment (p. 91).

Lucía's love and understanding goes to the point of self-sacrifice: she understands and even defends her husband Sergio when, out of frustration, he becomes physically abusive against her, and blames herself for his aggressiveness (p. 77). Terminally ill in the third act, Lucía is still protective of Sergio, not wanting to let him know that she is aware of her approaching death (p. 98). The depiction of Sergio's violent behavior towards Lucia, because she cannot bear his children, certainly contains a strong criticism of machismo. Nevertheless, Bortnik's description of the insensitivity and even violence of some men does not make her discourse feminist in the proper sense of the word. Rather than questioning gender role distribution itself, she blames the insensitive male for taking advantage of the nurturing, self-sacrificing and essentially passive woman. Even then, it is the deep frustration men experience that leads to their abusive behavior, which women, therefore, do not only suffer quietly, but, when they are as wise as Delia or Lucía, understand and forgive. Interestingly enough, the character with no social or political conscience, who, in consequence, is inmune to the bad conscience the other male characters experience, is also the most *machista*, and, as in Diosdado's *Olvida los tambores*, the scapegoat for anyone's ill will against male chauvinism. Angélica's husband Roberto continuously nags his wife in the first act (p. 39, 47). He displays characteristic macho attitudes towards women, judging them by their looks. He asks Sergio to admire his daughter Viviana's body: "¿Viste Vivianita qué bomba?" (p. 65). He suggests to Sergio that, now that his wife is "even more appetizing," he should make (and keep) her pregnant (p. 66).

Notwithstanding the criticism of sexist behavior apparent in this and other plays, Bortnik seems to replace the old Yin and Yang with a new one. Femaleness in *Primaveras* is defined as strong, peace-loving, nurturing and creative, terms that Toril Moi regards as equally essentialist and confining as the old feminine virtues they substitute. The following quote illustrates her point:

> It is after all patriarchy, not feminism, which has always believed in a true female/feminine nature: the biologism and essentialism which lurk behind the desire to bestow feminine virtues on all female bodies necessarily plays into the hands of the patriarchs. (124)

Bortnik's interest in women's issues is mirrored in almost all of her work. An advocate for women's rights, she addresses issues like sexism, violence against women, the tragedy of unhappy marriages where the partners pursue opposing ideals, female friendship, and the struggle for independence. Bortnik exhibits a strong sympathy for her female characters, whose lives and emotions are generally viewed in much greater detail than those of the male characters. Therefore, Bortnik's discourse is in many ways certainly feminist. However, the confusion of female and feminine in part of her work tends to reinforce stereotypical thinking patterns. Interestingly enough, this happens particularly in the plays where the realistic plot is laced with symbolism and allegorical elements, like *Papá querido*, *Primaveras* and *La isla*.

⚜

Although they are not plays in the strict sense of the word, I have included two screenplays in this discussion of Bortnik's work. Bortnik herself sees film and television as types of theatre that allow a wider and more simultaneous distribution (Introduction to *Papá querido* 25). This, of course, is a far too simplistic view, since the two genres differ in more than just spectator numbers. However, since I am concerned with content analysis and the relevance of theatre as a tool for social change, I feel it is reasonable to include two filmscripts in the discussion.

La isla, based on an idea by Bortnik and Alejandro Doria, is the only work in this discussion that has no discernible political content. What Couselo called the "intimate, poetic, and psychological" content of this script was in no danger of falling under the shears of a harshening censorship in 1979 (Couselo, Introduction vi-vii).

The central theme in *La isla* is the loneliness and alienation to which the human being is exposed in a cruel and violent world. The island of the title is the imaginary place of reclusion to which the protagonists withdraw when the outside world becomes unbearable for them. The island is also a symbol for the mental asylum where the action takes place, and where the protagonist, Soledad, finds a fragile protection from the world outside its gates.

Soledad is a young woman who refuses to grow up emotionally, owing to a traumatic childhood experience that is explained fairly late in the script. She lives in the fantasy world that the fairy tales she reads provide her. When the troubled Sebastián is brought to the asylum, for Soledad he is Sasha, the prince in Andersen's tale of *The Little Mermaid*. Through her dedication, Sebastián leaves his imaginary island and falls in love with her. Soledad is not happy with this change, since Sebastián's speech creates an obstacle between them. Frightened by his uncontrolled passion and completely disturbed by his final departure after her refusal to accompany him, she shuts herself off from her surroundings and withdraws to the island Sebastián had told her about. The final scene shows her, lost and lonely, lying on the edge of a stormy sea, symbol of her tormented self.

While *La isla* favors the perspective of the female protagonist, the script presents both men and women as victims. The female and male patients in the asylum are all equally tortured human beings. There is a difference, however. While the male patients are victims of their own frustrations and a general disillusionment with life, the female characters, both patients and visitors, often suffer the consequences of male violence or insensitivity, rather than from the effects of their own intellectual discontent. Magdalena's bitterness is linked to the fact that her husband slept with another woman while she was seriously ill (p. 154). Delia, who visits her husband Juanjo in the asylum, was almost beaten to death by him (p. 200). Soledad herself is a victim of her father's violence against her mother, Lucrecia (p. 201). Lucrecia's lies have caused Soledad to suppress those violent scenes, which now haunt her in her nightmares. The sleeping pills the patients get in the asylum are no remedy.

Men's anguish is rooted in the dreariness of everyday life, and in the harsh competition in a society that rewards the strongest and the fittest (p. 197). Michel, the poet who shares a room with Juanjo and Sebastián, eventually resorts to suicide in order to escape from a senseless life. Sebastián reads the poem he left behind which sums up the intellectual disenchantment with life that we find mainly in Bortnik's male characters. In a brief description of the Creation, the poet underlines the suffering the human being has to face from birth until death (p. 235).

Sebastián's trauma is his failure to fulfill the high expectations of his family and particularly of his brother. His brother, Alberto, had long ago left his parents' home, dissatisfied with his father's way of life. Having always admired Alberto, the latter's disappointment in him was a hard blow for Sebastián. His frustration closely reflects that of Carlos in *Papá querido* when he remembers the moment that his brother ceased to write to him (p. 227–28).

The narrowness of women's suffering, the reasons for which lie mainly in the cruelty of the men in their lives, contrasts with the much more transcendent reasons behind male frustration. The realm of women portrayed in *La isla* is the realm of domesticity. While this domesticity leads to neurosis for some of the characters, and women are shown to be trapped by their own submissiveness, the playwright, rather than questioning women's confinement, criticizes the cruel male-dominated world for not placing a higher value on those feminine qualities. While some female neuroses are directly linked to the narrowness of the traditional female role, the script seems to conflate description with prescription. Claudia is obsessed with cleanliness, and Magdalena has to struggle with the bitter feelings against her unfaithful and insensistive husband. Yet, when she sees how lost he is without her, she runs back into his open arms, disturbed by the look of abandon about him, as if he "didn't have anyone to look after [him]" (p. 208).

The character of Soledad also possesses many of the qualities that make up the cultural construct called femininity. She is nurturing, loving, dedicated, very shy, completely inexperienced in sex. She takes care of her collection of dolls and of her plants as if they were her children (p. 152). Sebastián's passion for her destroys the more or less peaceful world in which she has lived. His insistence on pursuing a sexual relationship ultimately destroys her trust in him (p. 229).

96

While Soledad is trapped on her island, there is another
character in the play who draws strength from her confinement.
Put into the asylum by a family that does not want to take care of
an old woman, Amanda, whom Soledad in the end confuses with
her long-ago teacher, Señorita Marta, is the wise woman who
repeatedly appears in Bortnik's plays. She embodies a poetical
perspective, like Clara in *Primaveras*. She understands and
accepts other people's behavior and feelings. She is the one who
provides Sebastián with a more profound perspective on the
loneliness of Soledad (p. 240). Her rebellion against the world
that has put her in the asylum is a quiet one. When her family
comes for the obligatory visit on Christmas Day, she asks Soledad
to push her in her wheelchair at running speed through the park
(p. 212). The reactions of the shocked family members satisfy her
deeply.

Amanda has the strength and the insight that none of the
male characters have. Michel, the poet who commits suicide,
knows a lot about both worlds, inside and outside, but he is
pessimistic and thus defeatist. The wise women in Bortnik's
work—Amanda, Clara, and also Natalia and Delia in
Primaveras—offer a view of reality different from that of the male
characters. While Clara and Amanda are helpless by a fast-
moving society's standard, they are spiritually strong. Though
marginal in the sense of their age and their handicaps, they are
really at the center of a world that runs in crazy circles, never
getting anywhere. While the role of the wise, contemplating
woman makes the female perspective a valuable one in Bortnik's
work, the question remains of how far this role of Earth Mother
reinforces female stereotypes. Bortnik's portrayal of women like
Amanda comes dangerously close to asserting that women's
immobility is acceptable—maybe even desirable—in the light of
their deeper understanding of history and nature. Nevertheless,
the plight of women in Bortnik's plays shows considerable
awareness of important problems in male-female relations, one of
which is lack of communication. In *La isla*, men and women live
in different worlds and speak different languages. Soledad
preferred Sebastián when he was quiet and introverted, because
he was speaking her language then (p. 180). Gregorio and Juana,

two patients in the asylum, talk without communicating, and seem perfectly unaware of it (p. 221). The difference in interests—Gregorio talks about public, Juana about domestic issues—indicates a basic problem in the relationship between man and woman, a problem Bortnik evidently criticizes here and in her other plays. Her response, however, does not often exceed an affirmation of feminine values against a world where male actions take society into dead end streets. The symbolic separation of male/masculine and female/feminine may provide a seductive contrast in highly allegorical plays, but becomes difficult to apply when Bortnik leaves the symbolic-allegorical realm.

La historia oficial, directed by Luis Puenzo (1985), is one of the commercially most successful films released in Argentina after 1983, and, like most popular films, subject of some controversy. Barnard argues that this film was aimed, both stylistically and thematically, at the national middle class and European and U.S. markets (61). Although this may be partly true, particularly in terms of the film's style—here Barnard points out director Puenzo's background in advertising—, Barnard does not do justice to its powerful criticism of the Argentine middle class and its passive role during the *proceso* years. Nevertheless, the film has also raised some criticism from within the movement of the *Madres*. In the newsletter *Madres de Plaza de Mayo*, Vicente Zito Lema writes that the message of the movie is directed towards "the most reactionary sectors, the blindest and the deafest." Among his objections, the most justified one, in my opinion, is that the film keeps silent on the fact that the search of the *Madres* and *Abuelas* did not limit itself to identifying the children of the disappeared, but also meant to find the people responsible for the atrocities (15). The filmscript is based on an idea by Puenzo, but was written by Bortnik, and finally revised by Bortnik and Puenzo for the final version (España 3).

Bortnik's name in Argentine television and film, and her authorship of the script for one of the most successful movies to come out of democratic Argentina, make it all the more surprising that Barnard completely overlooks her in his book on Argentine film. While he regrets the exclusion of women from the national film-industry, he never mentions Bortnik's name in his discussion of *La historia oficial* (Introduction ii).

La historia oficial is a complex film in terms of the wide variety of themes it addresses. The two main themes to be discussed here are the critical reconsideration of the role of the middle- or upper-middle class during the years of the *proceso* and the political awakening and emotional and intellectual emancipation of a female member of this class during the final moments of the Junta. Other related themes are the problems of child adoption, female friendship, and traditional marriage, all of which are tied together by the one recurring theme in Bortnik's work: the importance of being an active participant in one's social and political environment, and the condemnation of inaction.

Alicia, history teacher at a boys' preparatory school, wife of a businessman with close ties to the military government, and mother of the adopted Gaby, is forced by several events to abandon her comfortable passivity and question her marriage, her way of life, and, most importantly, her interpretation of history. Her road to political consciousness begins with her increasing suspicion that her daughter is one of those children taken away from their mothers in secret detention centers during the infamous "dirty war" in the late seventies. Her inquiries gradually reveal the mesh of self deception she and others had fabricated around her, and bring her into contact with the Mothers of the Disappeared. The story of her gradual and painful awakening is set in a time of great political turmoil in Argentina, when the loss of the Malvinas War provoked large popular outpourings against the military regime.

The film opens with a scene where the students and the faculty in Alicia's High School sing the national anthem. Alicia sings with conviction while in the rows of students there is a visible lack of enthusiasm (p. 15–16). The bad quality of the recording and the interference of police radio transmissions at the beginning of the film effectively subvert the government version of Argentine history.

Having always taught history from an uninvolved, acritical perspective, Alicia is shocked when some of her students start questioning the history books. Her anger reveals her fear that the seemingly safe world in which she lives, is a castle built on sand. Alicia's own words, which she automatically repeats at the beginning of each school year, take on their true meaning in the demand of the students to face and acknowledge the horrors of Argentina's current political scenario: "To understand history means being prepared to understand the world. No nation can survive without memory" (p. 17). The students confront her with newspaper clippings about the atrocities committed in the military's secret detention centers, particularly with the case of the "desaparecidos" (p. 61).

Deeply disturbed by the harrowing story of her friend Ana's detention and torture at the hands of the military, and by her students' insistence on historical truth, Alicia becomes more and more involved in the search for Gaby's biological parents. This search gradually deconstructs the "official story" and forces her to realize what the viewer suspects from the beginning of the film: Argentine society is not the unified, harmonious whole the regime wants the citizens to believe it is.

Alicia's awakening can be interpreted as the awakening of the middle class to a new perspective on the regime and its interpretation of history, which they so unquestioningly accepted. Barnard observes that the national bourgeoisies, seduced by the potential benefits to be gained from the military's economic policies, embraced the Junta and its political program, and turned a blind eye to the crass human rights violations (60). Although according to Barnard this is "noted only peripherally" in *La historia oficial*, the accusation against the passivity of the middle class is a central issue in the film, and is at one point spelled out directly. When Alicia asks Benítez about the truthfulness of the newspaper clippings, he indirectly accuses her of willful and comfortable ignorance, and, thus, of quiet complicity with the regime (p. 73). The film contrasts two Argentinas: that of the corrupt cohorts of the military regime, and that of the courageous and idealistic opposition. Alicia's social background and political immaturity place her on the side of the oppressors, making her insecure and confused. We see her looking on during a popular demonstration, separated from the protestors by the arms and helmets of the riot police. Conflicting feelings make her run into a side street. Not yet ready for the confrontation with the *Madres*, she chooses to look down on their silent march from a coffeeshop above street level, separated from their public display of grief by the comfort of the interior space (p. 74).

The film is an indictment of the complicity between the upper-middle class, international business, the Church, and the military. Alicia represents the most common of collaborators, those who closed their eyes and their ears to the atrocities committed by the military in the name of progress. She also embodies the traditional female role model, the wife who only knows the intimate, domestic side of her husband, and remains largely ignorant of his affairs in the public sphere, as businessman. Roberto is strongly reminiscent of the greedy, egocentric Roberto in *Primaveras*. Like him, he rose socially and financially while around him everything deteriorated. In a crucial dispute with his father and his brother, Roberto takes an anti-idealistic stance, reminding them of "their" defeat in the Spanish Civil War (p. 103). Roberto's confrontations with the inquisitive Alicia, the hatred he feels against her friend Ana, and his violence against everything and everybody who question his way of life, make him a wholly unsympathetic character. At the end, however, his loneliness and desperation show, in a typically Bortnikian fashion, that he is himself a victim. During the last tumultuous moments of the regime, he loses everything. The contacts he had in the government who were able to save themselves and disappear did so, leaving the less powerful behind to take the blame for all the shady operations in which Roberto is deeply involved (p. 130). The alliance between the upper middle class, embodied by Alicia and Roberto, and the military regime, has ultimately brought the former few benefits. In the moment of crisis, they were the first ones to lose. Alicia's sterility in this context may be interpreted as a symbol for the sterility of their unproductive and ultimately unstable position in Argentina's militarized society.

According to *La historia oficial*, the armchair criminals who supported the military's "process of national reorganization," and who could quietly withdraw from the scene when the regime crumbled, had strong ties to international business. The film makes a not so subtle point of the North American presence in Argentine business and politics. Roberto's departure to the United States in the company of the General and two businessmen, leaves no doubt as to who holds the reins in Argentine politics. The vehicles that escort them to the airport, Ford Falcons, infamous for their threatening presence on the streets of Buenos Aires during the dictatorship, complete the image of ruthless power behind the well-groomed surface of international business (p. 79). The attitude of the official Church in the time period between 1976 and 1983 is another target for the film's accusations. Father Ismael's unfriendly rebuttal to Alicia's inquiries about her daughter's birthplace, and his accusation that she has lost her faith in God, hint at the pact between the most reactionary institutions in Latin American society, and contain an open censure of the silence and complicity of the Church during the years of the worst human rights violations in Argentina (Fisher 53, 57).

The film, however, does not indicate in any way a new romantic liaison between the social class Alicia belongs to and the lower class of Gaby's biological family. Class creates a seemingly insurmountable rift between her and the Mothers of the Plaza de Mayo. The stoic Sara, likely to be Gaby's grandmother, with her tired face and her modest dress, contrasts vividly with the elegant Alicia. Sara's stoical attitude and her advice to Alicia not to cry, since she knows from experience that crying does not help, hinder the viewer from emotionally identifying too much, while at the same time foregrounding the immense suffering of those in a less privileged social position.

La historia oficial leaves no doubt about the difficulty of reaching social consensus in a country where the suspicion the middle class historically holds toward the working class, deepened by Peronism, made the *proceso* dictatorship possible in the first place. The script is much less clear in its exploration of gender difference and its role in politics. The film is certainly sensitive to women's issues.   Here an inquisitive woman confronts an overwhelmingly male system of oppression that embraces the public and the personal spheres. The emancipatory process for Alicia starts in her own home when she realizes that her moral convictions are not the same as her husband's. The questioning of the official truth she has always tacitly accepted leads her to question not only Roberto's political attitude, but also the trust she has placed in him as her husband, thus blurring the line separating the private and the public spheres. Alicia's initial reluctance to abandon her comfortable ignorance and the separation she tries to keep between the public space and her home, between the living history on the streets and its interpretation in her textbooks, in the end are impossible for her to uphold. The struggle on the streets invades her bedroom. The most innocent space, Gaby's room with its toys and cheerful colors, becomes a torture chamber when Roberto physically abuses her there (p. 133).

Alicia's search for the truth about Gaby signifies a definite step away from the women integrated into the Establishment. The wives of Roberto's colleagues, or Alicia's high school friend Dora, are models of negative female stereotypes. They consider politics to be the realm of men, and support, unquestioningly, the ideology of their husbands, and, by extension, of the military state. Dora embodies all those Argentineans who firmly believed that the disappeared had participated in "subversive" activities, and deserved punishment (p. 38). Alicia's quest is a lonely one, during which she has to face the feelings of guilt Roberto tries to stir in her for "abandoning" Gaby. Gaby's innocent confusion of words when she refers to Ana ("solitaria" for "solidaria") cleverly hints at the loneliness of the woman ostracized from her community either, paradoxically, for being a victim of political persecution, or for asking disquieting questions.

The political and economic brotherhood ruling Argentina rejects women's independence and solidarity with one another. Roberto's aversion toward Ana reflects the fear of female solidarity that is so vividly present in the efforts of the *Madres de*

Plaza de Mayo. For Roberto, women have to be adaptable, with no rough edges. His praise of Ana's (more feminine) looks, after her return from exile, is perversely ambiguous since he is aware of her terrible experience (p. 44).

Despite the feminist proposition that pins Alicia against a reactionary system based on male superiority, the script seems to fall into the traps of dominant discourse when it contrasts Roberto with Alicia's colleague Benítez. The only difference between them appears to lie in their opposing political convictions. Apart from these, the similarities are disquieting. They display an equally condescending attitude toward Alicia. While Roberto asks Alicia to stop thinking, Benítez's patronising and flirtatious behavior brings to mind equally traditional gender relations (p. 63). When Benítez commends Alicia for her new hairdo—she exchanged her strict bun for a more casual look—she replies that she looks like a crazy woman ("loca"). Benítez's ambiguous response ("It must be that I like crazy women . . . ") divests the term "locas," given by the military to the Mothers of the Plaza de Mayo in order to discredit them, of its subversive political meaning when it serves to identify the sexually attractive woman who "lets her hair down" (p. 112).

Benítez belongs to another "brotherhood" which, although liberal in its political views, marginalizes women in ways similar to those used in the party that wields the political power. In this context, it is important to look at the relationship between Benítez and his students, the same ones who challenge Alicia's assessment of Argentine history. They form a closely knit community, in which the feminine is ridiculed. Martín Cullen, a slightly "effeminate" student, is mocked by his classmates, and gets to play Vicenta in the reading of the classic *Juan Moreira* in Benítez's literature class. Gender roles are clearly defined: even in the liberal brotherhood men have to be *men*, and women have to be *women* in the traditional sense. In order to be accepted, Alicia has to become more feminine. We see her transformation from the strict, self-possessed teacher in the beginning, into a more tolerant and more attractive woman, who earns the goodwill of her students, and the admiration of her male colleague.

Alicia's departure at the end of the film could be interpreted as an unintended comment on the absence of a space for women in the public dialogue of the new democratic Argentina. Neither of the political camps has granted women a voice. The Mothers continue to march in front of the *Casa Rosada*, unwilling to be co-opted into political parties that ultimately are part of a system that does not value their voice. Their actions are thus much more politically subversive than the script for *La historia oficial* indicates. While the Mothers have succeeded in finding a public voice, and in "break[ing] away from the restraints imposed upon them by the myth of marianismo," the film does not do justice to this success (Fabj 14). It emphasizes the sentimental aspect of the search of the Mothers, rather than their demands for justice and retribution. While the male opposition in the film is very vocal (students, protesters, Benítez), the Madres are portrayed as sad and quiet. Forgotten is the very recent time of the Malvinas War when the Mothers were the only group to oppose it publicly (Fabj 10). In this respect the film seems to participate in the same endemic evil it attempts to criticize in its theme song about the land of forgetting, where no step is certain.

❧

Most of Bortnik's plays and scripts analyzed here link women's issues to political issues, which range from the discussion of the importance of moral values to concrete references to Argentine politics. However, Bortnik's call for breaking down the separation between the private and the public, and for establishing a link between individual responsibility and the political process, does not extend to the binary opposition of the sexes. Her plays *Papá querido* and *Primaveras* seem to indicate that women have a deeper understanding of the vital conflicts tearing apart Argentine society, and hold the key, if not for their solution, at least for a life in harmony with and in acceptance of human (male) frailty. The playwright seeks to rescue traditionally feminine characteristics from their marginality, and foregrounds the unique perspective that women contribute to a world in which the dominance of the male point of view has caused havoc. At the same time, she illustrates how, what she considers the innate nurturing qualities of women, have been ignored or exploited by men (*Primaveras*, *La isla*). In emphasizing the suitability of those characteristics defined by patriarchy as inherently female, Bortnik moves on dangerous terrain between description and prescription of certain narrowly defined gender roles. From a feminist viewpoint, this becomes particularly questionable when these roles inhibit women's stepping out of the private and into the public sphere. Only in the script to the film *La historia oficial* does Bortnik focus on one woman's attempt to do so, and even here the feminist reader and critic will find problems with the script's hesitant approach to the re-evaluation of traditional gender roles.

Bortnik's theatre and screenwriting critically explore Argentina's social and political reality. Her use of the rhetoric of liberal humanism and the recurring contrast between idealism and materialism as a key to the analysis of Argentina's political problems seem to make Bortnik more philosophically appealing than Gambaro. However, her characters' lucubrations on their personal broken dreams and the loss of a Golden Age idealism have less of an impact on the audience than Gambaro's visceral, gut-twisting approach. Gambaro's much more stylized theatre underlines the degradation of interpersonal relationships in an environment ruled and deformed by repression. Gambaro grants her female protagonists a much more radical role in the struggle against dictatorship than Borntik, questioning—particularly in her later work—the suitability of the image of the passive, nurturing female, when the space for this role has been restricted or has vanished in a brutalized environment.

Notes

[1] See Julia Kristeva's "Women's Time," and Toril Moi's "Feminist, Female, Feminine" in Belsey and Moore, *The Feminist Reader: Essays in Gender and the Politics of Literary Criticism*, 1989, 197–218, 117–32.

---

[2]Ellman takes these terms from Rebecca West's *Black Lamb and Grey Falcon*, New York: The Viking Press, 1964

Chapter Seven

Griselda Gambaro: The Political Pen and the Construction of a Feminist Perspective

Throughout the nearly thirty years of her career as playwright and novelist, Gambaro has been committed to the relentless analysis of her socio-political environment, dealing with what she terms "real facts" of Argentine life (Garfield 63). Whether the label worn by the political system of the moment was democratic or authoritarian, she has never ceased in her attempts to uncover the true face of repression, revealing the individual's fear of assuming responsibility and taking a stand against the gradual destruction of his or her freedoms.

Her earlier plays, like *Las paredes* [The Walls] (1963), *El campo* [The Camp] (1967), *La gracia* [An Act of Kindness] (1971), and *Información para extranjeros* [Information for Foreigners] (1973), in many ways foreshadow the excesses committed under the military rule of the *Proceso* years, while they are, at the same, time universal parables of human cruelty.

The years of the worst repression in Argentina (1976-1980) find Gambaro exiled in Spain, where Franco's death had just made the democratic transition possible. In this period, during which she published no new plays, she came face to face with the problems that literature encounters in a rapidly changing environment. During her stay in Barcelona she wrote *Lo impenetrable* [The Impenetrable], an ironic takeoff on pornographic fiction she did not attempt to publish in Argentina until 1984. According to Gambaro, literature has to respond to its socio-political context. She felt that in 1980, when she returned to Argentina, the time was not yet ripe for the publication of a novel that had been written with a more playful and permissive society in mind.

Gambaro has continued writing regularly in democratic Argentina. Her plays *La malasangre* [Bad Blood] (1981), *Del sol naciente* [Of the Rising Sun] (1984), and *Antígona furiosa* [Furious

Antigone] (1986), are testimony to her critical view of the political changes and her awareness of their possible futility.

Although Gambaro's work undeniably has a strong universal appeal, this study focuses on the relationship between her plays and the Argentine context, both in terms of their political content and in terms of her increasing preoccupation with women's issues.

The considerable amount of critical literature on Gambaro, who is internationally recognized and has aroused particular interest among North American scholars, tends to focus on two subjects: the experimental quality of her theatre, and the dialectic between victim and victimizer in her plays.

Gambaro's use of language and form has led many critics to place her next to French theatre of the absurd, something that has annoyed her very much (*"La difícil perfección"* 26).

The controversy between defenders of the "absurdist" theory and the "grotesque" theory (see below) has—perhaps pointlessly—occupied a large part of the literature devoted to Gambaro's theatre (De Toro 42). Neither in Argentina nor abroad has Gambaro escaped the dreaded pigeonholing. For thirty years now, due to the nature of her theatre but perhaps also due to her gender, she has been regarded as part of a vanguard movement, aloof from the other developments on the Buenos Aires stages. Director Alberto Ure writes that she was recognized, but also "cristallized," separated from other, officially accepted trends in the renewal of Argentine theatre (Ure 15).

The controversy about the classification of Gambaro's theatre serves us here to underline the close link between her work and Latin American or, more concretely, Argentine reality. Gambaro distances herself from the French absurd, because it seems too far removed from her immediate context as Argentinian (*"La difícil perfección"* 26). The link she sees between her work and the *grotesco criollo* is an indication of the degree to which her theatre is rooted in the Argentine experience. In her study of the *grotesco*, Kaiser-Lenoir describes the movement as characteristic of the Argentina of the early twentieth century, since it expressed the disillusionment of large sectors of the immigrant population. Leaving Europe with the hope to *hacer l'América*, many of the immigrants encountered hardship in a country where the economic growth at the end of the 19th century was showing the first signs of rapid decay. According to Kaiser-Lenoir, the *grotesco criollo* depicts the cruel contradiction between a miserable reality and the idealized image of it that man creates in order to ignore or transcend his misery, thus perpetuating an unfair status quo. The plays all end with the frustration of the characters' illusions and aspirations. Their self-delusion leads to an even more bitter revelation of the bleakness of reality when the masks finally fall. The divorce between language and gestures that reflects the impossibility to function like a human being in alienating circumstances, is something we find again in Gambaro's theatre. Here, however, the implications are different. Gambaro continues to analyze the individual in a hostile environment, but the sufferings of the victim are more often than not self-induced by his or her passivity and silent complicity with the oppressor. The victimized character never ceases to believe in the good will of the victimizer who hides behind a mixture of incoherent and conflicting messages that range from cruelty to a seemingly friendly and caring attitude. The disintegration of language as a means of communication, one of the most important characteristics of the *grotesco criollo*, surfaces again in Gambaro's theatre in the divorce between signifier and signified, and the incongruity between verbal expression and gesture.[1] This devaluation of language as a vehicle for understanding in all three types of theatre—the French absurd, the *grotesco*, and Gambaro's work—, points to a reality where the individual feels lost, alienated, or oppressed, be it by a universe devoid of order and divine providence, or be it by an excess of power exerted by an incomprehensible, cruel system. However, while in the European absurdist theatre resignation and self-obliteration generally precluded social protest,[2] Gambaro's theatre is more directly one for social change. Even during the bleakest moments we know that the characters could overcome their frightening circumstance if they fought their own passivity.

It probably is safe to say that a sense of the absurd is universal, and that, given the course of Argentine history since 1930, an Argentine playwright like Gambaro may have felt particularly inclined to express these feelings of absurdity in her work.

The victim–oppressor dichotomy is the central recurring theme in Gambaro's plays, and forms the other pole around which clusters an important part of the critical work.[3] Maris-Martini distinguishes two structural patterns (*subsistemas*) in Gambaro's work. The first one is based on "the dialectic between two acting principles: victimizing and being victimized" (Maris-Martini 28). In these plays the victim succumbs psychologically or even physically to the victimizer. Some titles are *Las paredes* (1963), *El desatino* [The Folly] (1965), *Los siameses* [The Siamese Twins] (1965), *El campo* (1967), *Sólo un aspecto* [Only One Aspect] (1971), and *Dar la vuelta* [Turn Around] (1972). The second *subsistema* adds a third component: rebellion. The victim rebels, often combining aggression and a capacity for tenderness (Maris-Martini 28). This group includes plays like *La malasangre* (1981), *Del sol naciente* (1983), and *Antígona furiosa* (1986).

Although both groups slightly overlap chronologically, Gambaro's later work has an overall tendency towards a more optimistic outlook. Gambaro herself speaks of a different, "more compassionate" optic in her latest plays (Interview with Betsko and Koenig 191).

Interestingly enough, this development in Gambaro's later work is accompanied by a more important presence of women protagonists. Women take on the role of rebels against a mostly male oppressive order. Although their rebellion is sometimes doomed to failure, their gesture points to a future less bleak. "Yo me callo," cries Dolores at the end of *La malasangre*, "pero el silencio grita" ["I remain silent, but the silence screams."] (p. 110).

Through the years, Gambaro has become a more and more outspoken advocate of a feminist perspective. While in 1980 she still denied having written from a male point of view in her earlier plays,[4] in 1986 she admitted being more familiar with the world of men, which she defined as the political world. Her awareness of what it means to be a woman in this world, came more recently, and peopled her plays with female (rebellious) protagonists (Interview with Magnarelli 130). Gambaro believes in a female aesthetic without relinquishing the independence of the literary work from its creator. Without clearly defining what this new aesthetic means for her, she states that women should try to make their vision "less shapeless" and different from the male vision (Interview with Betsko and Koenig 193).

This study focuses on the evolution of Gambaro's perspective from a predominantly male point of view to one that includes the female vision of Argentine reality, and of a society ruled by a hostile and alienating order in general. The first half of this chapter will deal with some of the plays that are structured around the victim-oppressor dichotomy. In these plays a possible rebellion is not yet envisioned, and the few women characters that appear conform to traditional gender roles. The second half encompasses some of the plays of Maris-Martini's second subsystem. Here rebellion becomes an increasingly important factor. The protagonists—victim and rebel in one—are predominantly female, although they do not completely relinquish their traditional roles.

All these plays demonstrate Gambaro's commitment to a theatre for social change. In her view, it is the genre's responsibility to provide a critical perspective at a moment when historical circumstances do not allow juggling with ambiguities ("La difícil perfección" 31).[5]

❧

Las paredes, written in 1963 and staged in 1966, is Gambaro's first play and combines many of the characteristics of her later work. Conceived towards the end of a time period (1955-1966) marked by a long struggle to find a civilian alternative to Peronism, Las paredes may be read as a parable about Argentina's dependence on authoritarian rule, and of the average citizen's lack of willpower to oppose a regime that leads to the eventual destruction of the individual.

A young man, the anonymous joven, finds himself in a luxuriously decorated room which gradually reveals itself as a prison cell. Confused by the contradictory remarks of his hosts, the *ujier* [custodian] and the *funcionario* [official], he feels compelled to accept the cell as a temporary dwelling, for an unclarified purpose. The lavishly furnished room becomes gradually barer and smaller in size. The Youth has entered a world where time and space are out of his control (Cypess 96). The more the room looks like a cell, the less the Youth seems willing to accept the reality of his imprisonment. He makes his jailers' words his own, becoming increasingly dependent on their will and whim, and stripping himself of the last remainders of his identity. Having completely lost his willpower, he finally sits down to wait for the walls to close in on him, unaware that the open door offers the possibility of escape.

Both in content and form, *Las paredes* sets the stage for Gambaro's future plays. The "dynamics of interaction between oppressor and victim," between the detainee and his jailers, are found in variations in most of Gambaro's work (Lockert 38). However, only in a few plays is there such a realistic reflection of what was to become the worst nightmare in Argentine history. The protagonist's unexplained detention, the obscure investigation of his identity by the official, the deliberate confusion he is kept in concerning his fate, are all rooted in a bleak reality.

Gambaro's masterful use of language and gesture is modeled after the distortion of language in a militarized society. *Las paredes* foreshadows experiences like the one of Timerman in Argentina's secret detention centres under the *Proceso*. His account of his jailers' cruel games with threat and hope shows how true to life the seeming absurdity of the play really is. Shortly after his arrest, the blindfolded Timerman was told by one of his jailers that he was going to be executed.

> No digo nada. Vuelve a hablar: "¿No querés decir tus oraciones?" No digo nada. Comienza a contar.
> Su voz es bien modulada. Es lo que se podría decir una voz educada. Cuenta lentamente. Pronuncia bien. Es una voz agradable. Sigo en silencio.
> (. . .) . . . diez. Ja . . . ja . . . ja. Oigo risas. Me pongo a reír también. En voz alta. A carcajadas.

[I don't say anything. He begins to count. His voice is well modulated. One could call it an educated voice. He counts slowly. He pronounces well. It is a pleasant voice. I continue to be silent. (. . .) . . . ten. Ha . . . ha . . . ha. I hear laughter. I also start laughing. Loudly. Heartily.] (10)

The cruel combination of threats and jokes, of hope and despair that leads the victim to the brink of insanity, is something frequently found in *Las paredes*. In a sequence strikingly similar to Timerman's account, the Custodian tells the Youth that they are going to cut his head off. His laughter is echoed by that of the Youth, whose reaction walks a fine line between histeria and the most abject dispair (p. 28).

Like thousands of illegally detained, the Youth is a "prisoner without a name" in a cell where an indefinite number of other people have stayed. Like the large numbers of *detenidos* and *desaparecidos* of the late seventies, whose detention was officially denied, the Youth was brought to his cell by armed men. His account of the detention is contradicted by the Custodian, who denies that his "guest" was forced to accompany those men, while at the same time admitting that he could not have resisted their "invitation" (p. 12). The "double-talk" Esslin singled out as a characteristic of the absurd, here, far from being devoid of any real meaning, is of a systematic nature, geared to destroy the prisoner's common sense. The Custodian and the Official work together in their attempt to manipulate and victimize their "guest." Their complicity becomes obvious when they exchange a wink after having staged a fight with the Youth (p. 34).

While in the beginning the Youth still protests against the rude replies of the Custodian, the Official's manners and fatherly concern for his well-being overwhelm him (p. 16). The elegantly dressed Official acts as the benevolent patriarch whose cruelty and dishonesty are all the more threatening since they are hidden behind smiles and soothing words. His attempt to manipulate the victim by alternately using threats and words of hope and consolation has its equivalent in reality. Perhaps the most frightening aspect of Timerman's experience was the apparently friendly gestures that alternated with the brutality of the torturing sessions. The torturer's inquiries after the well-being of the victim, the cup of coffee or the blanket offered, seem to spring from the need to underline the victimizer's absolute control of the victim's world (Timerman 41).

Expecting words to conform to facts and actions, the Youth is lost in an environment where these are in constant contradiction. When he discovers that the heavy curtains do not cover the expected window, but the naked wall of a prison cell, he is dumbfounded (p. 14). While he seems to suspect he is a prisoner, he is unable, and increasingly unwilling, to look beyond his "host's" misleading benevolence. Soon he starts to censor his own utterances, making them conform to the Official's in an attempt to please him and not to arouse his temper (p. 15). Trying to calm the outraged Official, the Youth admits, against his own better judgment, having imagined the weapons on the men who detained him (p. 16). He accepts the vague and contradictory explanations given for the screams of pain he hears coming through the walls (p. 17). Finally, he blames himself for being in the cell, and thus takes the responsibility from his jailers' shoulders. Giving up resistance against his situation, he loses his identity and ends up being a puppet abandoned to his oppressors' manipulations.

In his detailed study of the verbal tactics in *Las paredes*, Robert Parsons discusses the strategies Gambaro employs to create a menacing metaphor for the absolute control a capricious and tyrannical authority can exert over all aspects of the life of its subject. Language ceases to be a coherent system of communication and becomes a threatening labyrinth of illogical statements. The Youth is exposed to a never-ending stream of words that he has trouble interrupting or contradicting.[6] Not only is this stream of words in itself an instrument of power and intimidation; its content grows gradually more threatening. In the beginning, the Official only occasionally laces his discourse with threatening vocabulary. Thus his use of the word *ejecución* when he talks about a painting, acquires a harrowing ambiguity for the Youth (p. 14). Similarly, the Official plays with the word *muerte* [death] in an insincere attempt to console his prisoner (p. 19). Associated with the contradiction between verbal utterances is the contradiction between these and the actions and gestures of the oppressors. The Official's emotional outbursts and self-incriminations, and his benevolent, paternal remarks are in stark contrast with his real intentions. Having just assured the Youth of his good will, he steals his watch (p. 20). Like the Official, the Custodian starts out by trying to make the Youth feel at ease (p. 21). However, his gestures and words betray his intentions. He steals his victim's money and he beats him brutally when he notices his superior has already stolen his watch (p. 24, 45).

The allusions to a harrowing fate awaiting the prisoner become increasingly frequent as the play progresses. Seemingly innocent words acquire a dreadful meaning in a context heavy with suspicion and insecurity. After having been shaken by an increasing number of direct threats, he reaches the point where he refuses to accept the reality he has all along suspected to exist behind the smiles and insincere words of his "hosts."

The subversion of language in *Las paredes*, and in most of Gambaro's later plays, stands for the very real distortion of language and truth under the military governments in Argentina and other Latin American countries. Curiously enough, while the military leadership in Argentina was concerned about words not meaning what they represented, it—sometimes indirectly—introduced a type of newspeak that served the double purpose of deluding the citizens and of reminding them of the ubiquity of the military. During a speech in celebration of the *Día de la Armada* in Santa Fe, May 1977, Almirante Massera warned the public about the corruption of the Western world by subversive counter-cultures, a corruption which Argentina had the mission to stop. He blamed these supposed counter-cultures for subverting language in order to "invent a theology that justified violence" (Avellaneda, *Censura* II, 150). However, the military itself was responsible for semantic subversion when, through its actions, it indirectly created the term *desaparecidos*, or when it renamed the busstops in Buenos Aires *zonas de detención* in the late seventies (Piglia 98-99). The meaning of words that under the dictatorship acquired connotations bothersome to the leaders was manipulated in the yellow press. In their analysis of the mainstream women's press under the military and during the first years of democracy, Eduardo Varela-Cid and Luis Vicens point out the distortion of the meaning of words in two books on dream interpretation issued by the ultra-conservative *Para Ti* and *Vosotras* in 1984. Here are a few examples:

Uniforme: Llevarlo puesto indica gloria y celebridad
Cadáver: Verlo: casamiento o nacimiento en la familia o en personas de su amistad.
Urna: Verla es acontecimiento triste.
[Uniform: To see it being worn indicates glory and fame.
Corpse: To see it: wedding or birth in the family or among your friends.
Urn: Seeing it means a sad event.] (25-27)

Clarity was not exactly one of the prerogatives of the military when it came to speaking the truth. Of the press, only the *Buenos Aires Herald* preserved a certain amount of freedom, because it was in English (Graham-Yooll 107).   *La Opinión*, of which Timerman was the editor, was censored because in several occasions it had published information that had appeared in incomprehensible form in other newspapers, and had taken it apart word by word, explaining the true meaning (Timerman 23).

As Méndez-Faith points out, *Las paredes* unfolds its meaning in a contextual reading, which establishes an unmistakeable correlation between the Argentine nation and the prison cell (833). The Youth's passivity is similar to the inertia of many other people who think their life is secure when they go to the office every day, and spend their Sundays in the countryside. His last words before he sits down to wait for the walls to collapse on him are his stubborn assertion that he will take a trip to the countryside on Sunday (p. 58).

Several symbols in the play express the refusal of the Youth and of people in general to accept the existence of and confront an oppressive political system.   The lavishly furnished room the Youth is first led into is as much an expression of the jailers' deviousness as of the Youth's own wish to idealize his situation.[7]

The Youth's fear of causing trouble and changing his situation eventually leads to his destruction, just as the habit of acceding to others' demands literally causes the death of the protagonist in Gambaro's *Decir sí* [To Say Yes] (1978). The central symbol here is the doll that the Official's men confiscated when they raided the Youth's room. The Official and the Custodian bring the life-sized doll into the cell to keep the Youth company. The latter is horrified. He and his housemates had taken turns in keeping the doll, all of them unable to tell the landlady they did not want it (p. 39). It is interesting that the Youth and his former housemates are all referred to as "guests." The Youth is an *invitado* or a *huésped* ["guest"], his housemates are *huéspedes*. Their inability to assert themselves and take action relegates them to the status of guests in a country they should be able to call their own. Their lack of resistance makes them spineless like the Youth, who at the end of the play has, in Podol's words, "becomes as docile, rigid, and inhuman as the doll he holds on his lap" (46).

A tale of senseless cruelty and human passivity, *Las paredes* combines many of the dramatic techniques of Gambaro's subsequent work. It is a play that reflects a "man's world," as the playwright herself said about her early work in an attempt to justify the absence of women characters. This world is incomprehensible and unjust. The absence of women characters, according to the author herself, reflects women's very real absence from the public sphere ("¿Es posible. . .?" 21). However, despite Gambaro's effort to portray women's victimization in a patriarchal society under dictatorial rule, some of her earlier plays walk a fine line between representing inequality, and reinforcing traditional female stereotypes.

❧

El desatino [The Folly], written in 1965, was staged that same year at the Instituto Torcuato Di Tella, the Buenos Aires center for the avant-garde. In keeping with the cosmopolitan atmosphere, *El desatino* is less recognizably linked to its socio-political context, and more a universal tale of the human being lost in an incomprehensible world. Perhaps more readily interpretable along the parameters of French absurdism than some of Gambaro's other plays, *El desatino* still is steeped in the Argentine tradition of the *grotesco criollo*. It deals with loss of identity in a world where ideals of love and friendship are just illusions, the collapse of which causes self-annihilation.

Alfonso, the central character in *El desatino*, undergoes an experience similar to Gregor Samsa's in Kafka's *Die Verwandlung* (1912). Hampered in his freedom to move by a large metal object that has somehow become attached to his foot, he is confined to his bed and has to endure the cruel treatment of the people he should be able to rely on the most: his mother and his friend Luis. As in *Las paredes*, the protagonist's situation is in part self-inflicted since he fails to recognize the evil behind the friendly mask, and thus is unable to banish it. His dependency on his mother and his false friend, and his reluctance to accept the help of a stranger who attempts to remove the artifact from his foot lead to his demise even though the stranger in the end succeeds. Alfonso, incapable of literally and metaphorically standing on his own feet, is able to survive only in a relationship of dependency. Like the Youth in the previously discussed play, Alfonso gradually deteriorates from an initial attempt to get tools to help himself, to a loss of identity reflected first in his loss of speech, and finally in his death.

In this play, Gambaro employs the same verbal and visual techniques we have seen in *Las paredes*. The curtain opens on a set that at first glance suggests domestic banality: A sparsely furnished grey room, a cast iron bed, a chamber pot, and several wilted plants suggest a sordid, and yet realistic, environment. However, nothing is what it seems. Instead of getting up to face another dreary day, Alfonso realizes one of his feet is inmobilized by a large metal artifact. His initial shock quickly gives way to resignation, even conformity (p. 61).

The acceptance of the abnormal and its insertion into the banality of everyday life is what produces the absurdity in *El desatino*. The entrance of every new character awakens certain expectations in the reader or viewer that are quickly betrayed. As Karen L. Laughlin points out in her comparison of this play with Harold Pinter's *The Birthday Party*, Alfonso's mother appears at first as the stereotypical housewife complaining about her chores. Her complaints soon turn into a weapon against her son. She treats him with cruelty, exerting "her control even over his language, misinterpreting his words as well as his actions and continually turning them against him" (13). Alfonso's friend, Luis, from whom one would expect an effort to help, also betrays this expectation. His cruelty against Alfonso is less subtle than his mother's. It is reflected in the blatant contradictions of his utterances, and in his use of physical violence. The line between game and torture is blurred when he, at first playfully, ties a shawl around Alfonso's neck, and then slowly starts strangling him (p. 71). Although the entrance of his mother momentarily interrupts this escalation of violence, her words reinforce the nightmarish atmosphere when she assumes Alfonso is the initiator (p. 72). Like the Youth in *Las paredes*, Alfonso asks for forgiveness instead of reproaching Luis for his cruelty (p. 75).

In the second act, the difference between the elegantly dressed Luis and the deteriorating Alfonso becomes more marked (p. 81). Alfonso's mother and Luis have started an erotic relationship that strengthens their cooperation in Alfonso's victimization. The central subject of their verbal cruelty has become Lily, Alfonso's imaginary wife, whom he sees and talks to when he is alone. Both remind Alfonso that Lily does not exist. The mother, jealous of her son's concern for Lily, in the end controls this last remnant of Alfonso's independence. She organizes a party celebrating Lily's supposed pregnancy in a mockery of her son's fantasies and sexual frustration. Lily's last appearance in Alfonso's imagination reveals his inability to find sexual fulfillment with the woman of his dreams. It is in this scene, during his final conversation with Lily, that his speech begins to deteriorate (p. 96). Alfonso's dream starts collapsing because the girl-woman-vamp he himself has created is superficial, uncaring and, after all, just an illusion. When she finally says good-bye, she leaves to go to the movies with Luis, a defeat Alfonso himself has encouraged.

When in the final scene the mother invites the neighbors to celebrate Alfonso's fatherhood, he has already reached a state of indifference towards her cruelty, and even cooperates with her and Luis. In order to get rid of the *muchacho*, the young man who alone wants to be Alfonso's friend and has shown a true interest in Lily, he sends him to get a magazine (p. 99). Finally, Alfonso warns his mother and her guests when the Youth attempts to continue his destruction of the metal artifact (p. 104).

As Laughlin has pointed out, regarding the play's verbal strategies and its subversion of domestic banality, *El desatino* does have many similarities with the theatre of the absurd, particularly with Harold Pinter's "comedies of menace," and Artaud's "theatre of cruelty" (Laughlin 12). However, *El desatino* also belongs in the tradition of the Argentine *grotesco*. Alfonso may be compared with the protagonists in Armando Discépolo's plays, who try to deny an absurdly cruel environment by conforming to it until the mask does not hold up any longer and the terror of reality drives the characters into insanity or death.[8]

El desatino is not a political play in the obvious sense in which *Las paredes* is. Although the underlying message in both plays is a warning against passive acceptance of control over one's life, *El desatino* focuses on the most private, intimate sphere, the family. The implications of *El desatino* are thus more frightening. Not even the closest friends and family members offer any support. The environment we mistakenly believe to know best may prove to be more dangerous than the unknown which we regard with suspicion. We therefore turn out to be our own worst enemies, most easily controlled and manipulated when we trust the manipulator. Alfonso lets himself be manipulated by his mother, his friend, and his own perception of the ideal woman. Although it is his only expression of willpower, his imagination is not completely independent. Lily looks and acts like a sex symbol out of a North American movie. However, his vision of her is slightly distorted, a possible reference to the distortion of the Argentine cultural identity under the ubiquitous North American influence (p. 94).

The cultural invasion from abroad during the *proceso* years is an important, though little recognized, fact. Argentine radio and television seem to have been under extensive control of the U.S. broadcasting services, reflecting a presence of North American interests that will again be addressed in Bortnik's *La historia oficial*. Salas points out that a sizeable percentage of Argentina's foreign debt was contracted by television channels under the military regime (Salas 73). The presence of U.S. culture in Argentina also appears in other plays by Gambaro, often in grotesque distortion, a good example being the gangsters in *Dar la vuelta*.

While critical of tyranny, and of the passivity of its victims, the gender identification of these two interdependent roles is troublesome from a feminist viewpoint. Although the protagonist's situation is partly self-inflicted, and he several times becomes the victim of his own machismo, the play is written from an ultimately male perspective. This is suggested by the portrayals of the Mother and Lily, and of the protagonist's relationship to them.

Alfonso's mother embodies the prototype of the all-devouring matriarch, whose relationship with her son (and his friend and alter-ego Luis) has obvious oedipal overtones. In contrast to the other two main characters, she has no name. When Luis asks Alfonso for his mother's name, Alfonso, after some confusion, gives *Viola* as her name (p. 67). Although now, fifteen years after the first staging of the play, *Viola* may be understood as a reference to Roberto Eduardo Viola, president of the Junta in 1981, the name should be interpreted in a more general sense as a reference to her castrating effect on her son. She rapes ("viola") his identity, and will probably do the same with Luis, the other (male) character with a name. The final scene hints at a circular structure when Luis addresses her as "mother" after Alfonso has died (p. 105). This insatiable Mother or Female, who uses, abuses, and swallows her children or her mates, always remaining mysterious to them, acts like a regular housewife when she first appears on stage. Gambaro uses the stereotype of the nagging housewife (who, in the play's context, has no reason to complain, since she is the powerful one) to create the tyrannical figure that shatters the traditional expectations associated with the mother figure. The absence of the characteristic traits commonly linked to this figure—love, tenderness, support— seems to imply that these traits would be present in a society more just. Her ill treatment of her son inevitably brings to mind the opposite stereotype. Against the image of the overbearing and jealous mother on stage rises the image of the selfless, nurturing woman. From a feminist point of view, this is a questionable reinforcement of traditional gender stereotypes. Alfonso's mother combines all the negative traits traditionally associated with the domineering mother or mother-in-law. She wants Alfonso to be dependent on her and uses her own physical ailments to achieve this dependence (p. 63). She is jealous of the imaginary Lily and uses and destroys the gifts that Alfonso has bought for her (p. 64). Like the North American woman of Betty Friedan's *The Feminine Mystique* (1964), she wants to be girlish and young, a child-woman. She acts "aniñada," girlishly, with Alfonso and Luis, and dances around in her nightgown, imitating the imaginary Lily (p. 87, p. 97). Her repeated efforts to rejuvenate her appearance make her seem even more ridiculous (p. 76).

Lily, a vivid contrast to the mother, combines another set of stereotypical traits. When Gambaro was asked about her intentions in the stage directions which describe Lily as "An exaggerated version of a movie sex symbol," she justified this description with her attempt to reflect the stereotyped vision of a particular male character (Betsko, Koenig 194). However, the fact that Alfonso loses Lily—his only expression of freedom—because of his unassertiveness or, rather, his lack of machismo, casts a doubtful light on Lily's image as the sole projection of his imagination. Lily abandons Alfonso because he acts unassertively towards her. He accepts her refusal to sleep with him, and lets her go to the movies with Luis, knowing his friend will approach her sexually. This gesture, which under different circumstances could be interpreted as a generous one, here becomes another step toward his final destruction. His lack of assertiveness is really a lack of machismo in the most traditional sense: he is dependent on his mother, he is subservient to Lily, and he accepts being made into a cuckold by his best friend. "Sé hombre," ["Be a man"] says Luis to him (p. 71). But Alfonso is really not "man" enough since he lets himself be victimized by women.

As Cypess points out, "sexual proclivity in *El desatino* seems to function as an expression of free will" (98). The only character who in the end keeps her free will is the mother. Luis, the archetypal macho who constantly pinches the mother's behind, in the end is also subjugated by the mother. By losing his status as lover and assuming that of son, his independence starts diminishing. Female and male sexuality are viewed differently in this play. The mother's sexual activity is presented as another *desatino*. Her erotic games are portrayed as decadent because of her age and ugliness. Repeatedly we hear her "risita erótica y senil," her "little erotic and senile laughter" (p. 84). In contrast, Alfonso's pathetic desire for Lily has positive connotations since she represents for him the possibility of liberation and control over his own life.

The only strong and honest character in the play, the *muchacho*, has an attitude toward women and sex presented as normal and healthy. He is independent from women. He does not care whether he and his girlfriend fight, since "there are little chicks everywhere" (p. 88). He does not have an obsession, because he is free to pick and choose (p. 105). These discrepancies between the portrayal of the female and the male characters in regard to their sexual conduct, together with the traditional view of the role of the women characters, originate in a male perspective. The playwright's vision of gender will gradually change from an ultimately male point of view towards a more decidedly feminist outlook.

In *Dar la vuelta* [Turn Around] (1972/73), Gambaro expresses concerns similar to those in *El desatino*. However, the playwright here begins questioning the authenticity and appropriateness of traditional women's roles. The portrayal of women as victims of a sadistic authoritarian order reveals that their femininity is socially constructed.

In *Dar la vuelta*, the *patrón* ruthlessly rules his mob of grotesque caricatures of Hollywood gangsters: Mario *el Confuso*, Johnny Egg, Narciso *el Turco*, and Joe. The Boss incarnates the aggressive power behind the smiling mask. The incongruity of his actions and utterances intimidates and manipulates the "boys," who—for fear of their lives—accept low or no pay for dangerous jobs like robbery and extortion. Escape is impossible since every attempt to separate from the group is punished with death.

The action evolves around Joe, the victim–protagonist, and Valentina, his lover. They both nourish thoughts of rebellion. While Joe is mutilated to the point of becoming a shapeless mass without arms or legs—a reflection of his loss of identity—, Valentina and her children are executed after she decides to leave the group. Although Valentina is a very important character, her importance rests primarily upon her role in Joe's degradation by the Boss. The Boss uses Molly, the other female character in the play and a typical gangster-moll (hence the name), to subject Joe to his will and whim. He enjoys mortifying Joe by forcing him to act as Molly's husband, and to neglect and deny Valentina, his true love. Although Molly and Valentina are complete contrasts concerning their physical appearance and their personalities, they both are projections of the male imagination: Molly is a caricature of the conventional vamp from the Hollywood of the 1930's and 1940's, with a husky voice and enormous breasts; Valentina, on the other hand, embodies the shy, frumpy, motherly type. While Molly is vicious and unfaithful to Joe and sleeps with the Boss, Valentina has eyes only for Joe, and suffers quietly when he is unkind to her. When she first appears on stage, she drags a large sack behind her in which she hides her youngest baby, one of the many she keeps concealed at home. Her shyness, subservience, and her love for her children are indicative of the qualities destroyed in the world she lives in. Joe's feeble attempts to protect her are thwarted by the Boss and his boys, a false "brotherhood" held together by its belief in the superiority of the *macho*. In order to belong to this brotherhood, Joe is forced to assert his masculinity (p. 16).

Gambaro up to a certain degree deconstructs gender stereotypes, both male and female. Joe's machismo has fissures. He has trouble reconciling his own true feelings with the tough talk he is forced to use in this environment. When Valentina appreciates his kindness to her and tells him "sos bueno," ["you are good"], Joe immediately hardens again. He drags her, sick with nausea from another pregnancy, to the next job for the Boss (p. 32).

Joe's philosophy is to swim with the current: unable to free himself from his milieu, he wants Valentina to resign herself to the circumstances (p. 28). His failure to rebel against the discourse of power and machismo dictated by the *patrón* leads to his final degradation. Owing to his lack of will, Valentina has to die. It is here where, from a feminist viewpoint, the play's most important flaw lies. Valentina's rebellion is doomed to failure because she and her children are abandoned by the male. It is significant that Valentina's reason for wanting to quit the "milieu" is her wish to marry and to let the children, which she is hiding out of shame, out in the open (p. 47). She wants to lead a "normal" life, which here means having a family. Valentina tells the Boss she is marrying someone who is also leaving the mob. We would expect Joe to be the bridegroom. However, on her wedding day Valentina is alone with her children and the gangsters who have come to punish her.

Valentina is the character most true to herself. But as a woman and a mother she seems not to have the power to succeed. She is caught in a web of dependency, first on the mob, then on marriage. Both times she fails to be happy because men are either cruel or cowardly, and the only woman in a seemingly powerful position does not manifest any solidarity.

Molly acts viciously towards Valentina. She hits the bag where Valentina conceals her baby (p. 14). She tears up the dress she lent Valentina, accusing her of having destroyed it (p. 22). However, Molly's powerful position as the Boss's lover does not last. She is quickly removed from her pedestal when the Boss needs another slave for his criminal enterprises after Valentina's death. As swiftly as Valentina had been changed from a mouse into a vamp by means of a wig and artificial breasts, Molly is stripped of her only attributes of power. Johnny Egg and Mario *el Confuso* cut off her breasts in an unusually gruesome representation of women's subjugation (p. 57).

Women's sexuality in this play is arbitrarily pronounced or suppressed, depending on the use to which their bodies are put.

When Valentina goes to work with Joe, she dresses up as Molly. During the bank robbery she sits in the car exposing her breasts to distract the guards and possible witnesses (p. 15). Another job involves the extortion of a North American whom she has to lure with red underwear (p. 29). Joe participates in this sexual exploitation. His treatment of Valentina gradually worsens, paralleling his loss of identity. The fine line between sex and violence becomes increasingly blurred (p. 40, 42). After Valentina's death, he is satisfied with surrogates. Completely crippled after being run over several times by the other gangsters, he anxiously licks Molly's severed breasts (p. 65).

The political commentary is summarized in the final, ironic song which includes us readers and spectators in its criticism of our lack of resistance to the evil forces that, little by little, divest us of our freedom.

Dar la vuelta draws a connection between political and sexual exploitation. While the female characters here are still powerless, Gambaro's portrayal of the creation and destruction of female images by male power will eventually lead to the truly rebellious woman character who defies her traditional role in order to confront the oppressive political system.

આ

The objectification of woman in patriarchal society, one of several issues addressed in *Dar la vuelta*, becomes the central theme in *El despojamiento* [The Stripping] (1974). Like *Dar la vuelta*, this short one-act play uses stripping as a symbol for the female character's loss of dignity and identity. However, *El despojamiento* transcends the scope of the previously discussed play by disclosing the shattered humanity of the exposed and victimized woman. Her words are the only ones heard during the play, and although her speech is powerless against the powerful silence of the other (male) character, her utterances reveal a non-stereotyped, tortured identity. In this play marriage and motherhood are stripped of the qualitites of tenderness and hope hinted at in

Valentina's aspirations in *Dar la vuelta*. While Valentina mirrors the image of the naive and docile woman who faces her destruction with a smile on her face, the smile freezes on the lips of the woman in *El despojamiento* (181). She becomes conscious of her own pathos.

El despojamiento can be read as an ironic takeoff on a one-woman show, in that it places the actress centerstage only to divest her of the power commonly associated with such a public position. The protagonist turns from the aspiring actress, anxiously waiting for an audition, into the displayed object, without ever assuming the active role she seeks.

The anonymous character, the Woman, sits in the waiting room of a director with whom she is scheduled to have an interview for a job as actress or model. While she waits, she is gradually stripped by a young man—the silent *muchacho*—, a character whose behavior is described in the stage directions as impersonal and completely indifferent to the woman, whom he treats as another object (p. 172). Her attempts to transcend her objectification are all in vain since she uses a language and a set of gestures that patriarchy has created for her and that reinforce her passivity. She has been coerced to act a role in the society she lives in, where being young and sexy is absolutely indispensable for a woman. Her wrinkles, her used and borrowed clothes, contrast with her effort to seem young and seductive. As Becky Boling points out in her perceptive analysis, the "clothes worn underscore the concept of 'representation'" (60). The borrowed cape is supposed to make the woman look elegant (p. 173). She claims her shoes are new and expensive (p. 175). And when the young man brutally tears one earring from her ear, she is worried "they" will notice they are fake (p. 175).

"They" are the anonymous judges of her suitability for certain roles. She has no influence on the final decision, which we assume is made based on the pieces that the young man wrests from her. "Why don't they come and see all of me?" is a rhetorical question since nobody is interested in her as a human being. She has to wait patiently until it is "her turn," thus complying with the passive role expected from her (p. 175).

The roles she will have to play—if the unseen judges concede her a role at all—are limited, and have in common their demeaning effect on her as a human being. She remembers her first roles as ingénue, and now wonders if they will want her to play a prostitute. She believes she is well suited to play all types of mothers, "locas, cariñosas, distinguidas." Ingénue, mother, or prostitute, all three are projections of male imagination and desire which she is willing to portray, as long as they hand her the script (p. 180). Her performance is passive and uncreative, and the constant self-evaluation to which she subjects herself is done through the eyes of patriarchy. John Berger writes in *Ways of Seeing* that women have been trained to look at themselves through the eyes of men, thus turning the surveyed female self into an object (47). Gambaro's protagonist has internalized male discourse to the degree that she looks at and judges herself from the male point of view. This self-awareness and self-censorship extends to her use of language: "Maybe they want a who. . . a prostitute" (p. 180). And, as Boling points out, she appropriates her husband's or lover's voice by using frequent interjections addressing herself as her husband always does (Boling 63): "If Pepe saw me. 'Careful with what you're going to do . . . '" (p. 177).

Everything in life has failed the protagonist of *El despojamiento*. The words and gestures she has learnt are not appropriate any more. Gambaro's character looks for guidelines that would tell her how to behave when she realizes she is stripped of the attributes she needs to succeed in this society (p. 178) When she crumbles in the end under the certainty of the emptiness in and around her, her smile freezes, and she utters her last word: "¡Pepe!" (p. 181).

Her time in the waiting room becomes a metaphor for a life spent waiting for something wonderful to happen. The protagonist's optimism becomes gradually more difficult to uphold since the men around whom she has centered her life, have failed her. The rebellious undertones that every now and again surface in her monologue reveal a deep frustration with a life in which the role of the ingénue leads directly to a married life marked by abuse (p. 176). Her failure lies in the inability to recognize that for her there has been no difference between the mask and the self. Her hope for a new role keeps her trapped in the same cycle of self-denial that began when she accepted the role of the ingénue, since those roles, and her anxious waiting reinforce her dependency on a social order that is oppressive to her.

El despojamiento is probably the most outspokenly feminist play in Gambaro's repertory, since it deals specifically with the exploitation of women by the patriarchal order. Interestingly enough, it is not here but in the plays with obvious political overtones that women become active rebels. However, their protest is not a personal one, directed specifically against women's victimization by men. In this sense, *El despojamiento* remains unique within Gambaro's work. Rather, Valentina becomes Antígona, the angry denial of the possibility of love in a world ruled by despots, and the relegation of issues considered personal to the background until the moment when circumstances permit them to be considered "issues" again.

In *Del sol naciente* [Of the Rising Sun] (1984) and *Antígona furiosa* [Furious Antigone] (1986), women become agents of rebellion against a repressive system. Their struggle mirrors the struggle of thousands of Argentine women in the late 1970's and the 1980's in that, while not concerned specifically with gender issues, it creates a visible space for a more public role for women.

Del sol naciente, a one-act play in seven scenes, was first staged at the Teatro Lorange in Buenos Aires in 1984, directed by Laura Yusem. Although two years later Gambaro declared that the war alluded to in *Del sol naciente* could be any war, the play contains clear references to the 1982 crisis of the Falklands or Malvinas, occasioned by the Argentine military government's invasion of the disputed islands (Interview with Magnarelli 123).

As the title indicates, the play is set in the Land of the Rising Sun, a setting which fulfills a double purpose. On one hand, it removes the action from Argentine soil, thus creating the alienating effect necessary to judge more objectively. On the other hand, the "Rising Sun" may be a reference to the hope for change in a country haunted by dictatorship. Here the "Orient" would form the opposing pole to the *Occidente*, hailed by the members of the Junta as a sacred concept Argentina had the mission to defend. Massera called the *Occidente* "una actitud del alma" ["a deeply rooted outlook"], endangered by communist subversion. According to Avellaneda, the discourse used by the Proceso rationalized and justified the repression with the necessity to defend the so-called "Spirit of the West" ("*Argentina militar*" 20).

A third interpretation of the title could regard the Far Eastern setting as a symbolic reference to the protagonist's initial aloofness from reality. Suki is a courtesan, "distant and beautiful," who spends her days sitting in her exquisitely empty house, listening to the spaced tones of her string-instrument (p. 113). The only contact she has with the outside world is through her housekeeper, *Ama*, a character whose simpleminded humor and practical interests are strongly reminiscent of the *gracioso* of Spanish Golden Age drama.

Suki is passive. She does not want to leave the house, relying entirely on her housekeeper for news from the outside, in which she is, in any case, not very interested. During the play Suki gradually grows more aware of the frightening reality outside, the manifestations of which she tries to deny in the beginning (p. 114). Gambaro uses authentic *haikus* to express Suki's distorted poetic vision of reality rather than to create a play along the lines of Asian theatrical forms (Interview with Magnarelli 123).

The only interruptions of Suki's quiet lifestyle are the visits of the warrior Obán, the epitome of the traditional male. The housekeeper, seduced by his imposing presence, announces his arrival to Suki, stressing his military and sexual prowess: "How beautiful he is, my lady! . . . Iron the sword and iron the . . . (she ends with an allusive gesture)" (p. 116). Obán wants Suki's favors, which she is increasingly unwilling to grant him. In contrast to the housekeeper's naïve admiration, Suki questions Obán's egotism and his violent behavior.

The relationship between Suki and Obán deteriorates parallel to Suki's acknowledgement of the misery outside. The hungry and sick that roam the streets come to her door demanding the attention she has so far denied them. Obán's attempts to chase them away or to kill them are useless. They always come back. In the second half of the play, the hordes of the hungry are increased by the forgotten victims of the war in which Obán has participated. Their invisible ghosts roam the streets (p. 138). Oscar, who represents these despised and forgotten victims, intimates that they have come for more than just food. Reluctantly, Suki accepts his presence, moved by his childlike appeal for protection. Obán, on the other hand, repeatedly tries to kill him, angry that the dead want to have a voice (p. 150).

No doubt is left about the allegorical character of this play. Obán, the *samurai*, embodies the military leadership that subjugated Argentina, treating her like a prostitute, taking with violence what she would not give graciously. The failure of the invasion of the Falklands, the last attempt of the military to save face in front of a public increasingly dissatisfied with the ravaged economy and the suppression of personal freedom, triggered the final rebellion. Gambaro implicitly criticizes the reasons for the war, which served no purpose other than to boost the military's image in Argentina, distracting from economic misery at home. Suki, representing an Argentina increasingly critical of its leadership, reproaches Obán after his return from the war for the many senseless deaths fighting for land that could have been won by different means. Her reference to the "usurpadores usurpados" ["usurped usurpers"] who occupy the contested region, contains the playwright's criticism of the British claim to the Falklands. This claim had already been questioned in a 1965 United Nations resolution that affirmed that the islands were subject to decolonization, thus implicitly acknowledging Argentina's sovereignty (Rock 380). Suki's conviction that peaceful methods would have been more successful hints at the possibility of a diplomatic solution that could have been negotiated concerning the windswept islands. The military's misguided handling of the situation is directly reflected in Gambaro's play. The irresponsible conscription of ill-trained teenage boys for this war by the Argentine military is reflected in a scene in which Suki counters Obán's complaint about the inexpertise of the soldiers by reminding him of their unfair disadvantage in the face of their well-armed and well-trained opponents (p. 134).

Obán's affirmation after the loss of the war that "a battle is not the whole war" is an almost literal rendering of General Camps' words after the demise of the military government. In his interview with the Spanish journal *Pueblo*, in February of 1983, he expressed pride at his role in the defeat of subversive activities in the Buenos Aires area, congratulating himself on the defense of the West: "But the struggle is not over" (*Censura* II, 236–37).

Yet another scene closely mirrors the events in Argentina after the loss of the Falklands War. The outraged Obán tells Suki about a speech he gave to the people, a speech that ended in a riot (p. 149). Rock reports that on June 15th, 1982, when Galtieri made his final address to the Argentine people, violent clashes errupted on the *Plaza de Mayo* between the disenchanted populace and the police (381).

In a somewhat simplistic way, Suki embodies the abstract concept of the Argentine nation, of which the housekeeper is also an important part. *Ama* incarnates the sector of the population easily seduced by the rhetoric of the military leadership, and more concerned with its immediate well-being than willing to look behind the image of strength of its leaders. Appropriating Obán's rhetoric, she disapproves of Suki's generosity towards the hungry, and, although she is horrified by Obán's request, buries the victims of his atrocities, thus becoming an accomplice to his crimes (p. 151; 160).

In the portrayal of the housekeeper, Gambaro presents a somewhat aristocratic view of Argentine society. *Ama* dumbly admires Obán, following his orders blindly, just as large sectors of Argentine society believed in the military government and supported its venture into the Falklands. She is interested in preserving the status quo, and therefore also wants Suki to remain unchanged. When in the final scene Suki takes off her fancy kimono, her make-up, and her wig, *Ama* is shocked and disappointed by the changed appearance (p. 161).

When Suki, in the ultimate act of rebellion against Obán, hugs Oscar to console him and give him the peace he has been looking for, she has stopped being a courtesan (p. 163). In response to her promise that she will never again deny him, Oscar recognizes her as his mother (p. 163).

The feminism contained in *Del sol naciente* does not reside so much in the rejection of traditional gender roles as in the use of these as agents of social change. Suki takes advantage of her role as Obán's lover to question his actions. And when she finally assumes the role of mother of the lost and forgotten, this should be read as a subversive act rather than as obeisance to a confining definition of the traditional role. The political allegory unfolds around one woman's struggle for freedom from an oppressive relationship. Suki's act of stripping herself of all confining embellishments that have made her an object for Obán's pleasure is an act of rebellion against patriarchy. Her own freedom is, however, not an individual pursuit, but is directly linked to the redemption of the forgotten victims of Obán's cruelty.

Gambaro does not question the image of woman as nurturer, but she does reject her traditionally passive role, and at the same time issues a strong criticism of the sex-role ideology promoted by the military state. Gambaro ridicules Obán, whose name inverted reads *nabo*, with the double meaning of "stupid" and "penis" (Ure 19). Obán is a coward who, despite his pompous, violent behavior, shrinks from the sight of the blood of Suki's menstruation (p. 154).

While in *Del sol naciente* the struggle of the symbolic woman-nation outweighs the struggle of the woman-feminist, Suki's actions integrate her into the national process as avenger and redeemer, thus ending her seclusion and isolation.

❧

Sophocles' tragedy *Antigone* has often been adapted in Latin American theatre. *La pasión según Antígona Pérez* (1968), by Puerto Rican playwright Luis Rafael Sánchez, and *La joven Antígona se va*

134

a la guerra (1969), by Mexican author José Fuentes Mares, are only two examples of a significant repertory inspired by the Greek original. In the Latin American context, Antigone's rebellion against her uncle, Creon, can be easily interpreted as metaphor for the rebellion of the oppressed against dictatorship.

Antígona furiosa (1986) is a fairly close adaptation of Sophocles' tragedy. In Sophocles' work, Oedipus' sons Eteocles and Polyneices had arranged to rule Thebes by turn. When Eteocles refused to yield Polyneices his turn, the latter marched against his own city. Both brothers were killed, and the regent Creon ordained that, while Eteocles should receive honorable burial, Polyneices' body should be cast out unburied. Polyneices' sister Antigone contravened this order and suffered martyrdom in consequence (Hadas 80).

Gambaro's play opens where Sophocles' ends: Antígona has committed suicide by hanging herself, but wakes up again to re-live, in a series of nightmarish scenes, the events that caused her to take her own life. The play, first staged in 1986 at the Goethe Institute in Buenos Aires, blends Greek tragedy and Argentine reality in order to issue a passionate critique of tyranny as well as of Argentina's rush to put behind it a past Gambaro feels should not be forgotten.

The divergences from the original in Gambaro's version elucidate its political significance against the Argentine background. This Gambaro achieves not only by the double meaning the content acquires in the Argentina of the early eighties, but also by means of the Brechtian *V-Effekt*. The characters slip into different roles, Creonte being just an empty carcass into which the *Corifeo* steps to assume the tyrant's role, thus suggesting that tyranny is a dangerous and difficult to remove institution. Antígona also plays the roles of her sister Ismene and her lover Hemón. All characters continuously step out of their roles to comment on the events, thus fulfilling a role similar to that of the chorus in the Greek tragedy. This exchange of roles and the metatheatrical elements in *Antígona furiosa* create the alienating effect Brecht found to be an important tool in eliciting the audience's intellectual participation.

Sophocles presented Creon as a thorough, if inflexible ruler whose emphasis on duty and obedience was deemed necessary for effective government. His reasons for accusing Antigone were as wise as were Haemon's for defending her. Creon's one tragic error was his lack of compassion and his unwillingness to yield in Antigone's case, an error that led to the death of his son and his wife. Antigone's suicide in the prison in which she had been left to die compelled Haemon to take his own life, which in turn caused his mother's suicide. Creon was truly shaken and repentant, willing to die the death he had chosen for Antigone.

In contrast, Gambaro's Creonte is an entirely unsympathetic character who is unable to learn from his mistakes. Doubt is cast on his sorrow at Hemón's death, and on his wish to suffer incarceration, when Antinoo expresses bewilderment: "He is still powerful. Prison? What does he call prison? . . . The reverences and the ceremonies?" (215). Creonte's shamefaced admission that the throne and the power are still his, reflects the reality of the Argentine military's continued influence on public life after 1983.

In December of 1986, President Alfonsín signed the so-called *Ley del Punto Final*, which set a time limit on new prosecutions of military officers. In Fisher's account, Alfonsín's action caused the courts to accelerate the proceedings against military officers before the deadline expired in April of 1987. This, in turn, led to a series of rebellions in military establishments across the country. The government finally agreed to cease the prosecutions of military officers on active service. This, together with the *Ley de obediencia debida*, which officially limited responsibility for human rights violations to the top generals, was a major concession of a constitutional government in the face of a military still frightfully powerful (Fisher 146). Although *Antígona furiosa* was staged in September of 1986, a few months before Alfonsín's significant decisions, the play reflects the climate of fear and insecurity that led up to the army rebellions three months later. A self-confident military shows its face everywhere. In regard to the media, Salas points out that the majority of the radio and television stations are still indirectly controlled by the military, which explains the lack of coverage of the military trials on radio or television. According to statistics, the ministers of the military dictatorship are interviewed five times more often than those of the new elected government (Salas 70). The Mothers of the Disappeared, together with everyone else critical of the government, are expected to go back home and to keep quiet (Fisher 145). Carmen de Guede, one of the *Madres*, says that Alfonsín defamed the movement abroad, by telling journalists that the Mothers were "outside democracy" (Fisher 143).

From the point of view of Creonte, Antígona is the sister of a terrorist. To an Argentine audience, the parallels between Antígona, with "folly in speech, and frenzy in the heart," and the *locas* of the Plaza de Mayo, are obvious (Sophocles 95). Antígona is *loca*, crazy, because she demands the impossible. The *Corifeo* demands that "that crazy woman" be killed since she dares to remember the dead (p. 200).

The murdered Polyneices of the Greek tragedy becomes a collective of victims in Gambaro's adaptation. Like Suki, Antígona feels responsible not just for her brother, but for all victims. For her, love is more important than obedience to the tyrant. However, love is not possible in the world she lives in. Although born to love, she recognizes that hatred rules, and takes her own life "con furia" ["with fury"] (217). Antígona's death and her resurrection at the beginning of the play, when she removes the rope with which she hangs herself in the end, become a sign for the struggle against tyranny. Her refusal to die echoes the symbolic demand of the *madres*—"aparición con vida"—who insisted on the reappearance of the family members alive, when in all probability they had been murdered.

Antígona furiosa is Gambaro's comment on the democratic development in Argentina, which she regards with skepticism. Argentina's spring is still infested with the ugly reminders of the past, symbolized in the play by the ominous caws of invisible birds and disgusting droppings that fall from the sky (p. 213–14).

Like her Greek model, Antígona is a threat to institutionalized (male) power. In Gambaro's play, Creonte favors submissiveness in women, and rejects being commanded by a woman: "Women do not fight against men!" (p. 204). His attitude toward his niece is a direct reflection of the sexism Fisher observes in the attitude of the Argentine junta towards the *Madres*, namely, that they fell prey to their own misjudgement of the strength and determination of the women (Fisher 60). Antígona's death, far from being a defeat, is only the beginning of a never-ending revolt.

Antígona furiosa contains a strong feminist message that ties woman's fate to the welfare of the community, and has the protagonist draw strength out of her traditional role as sister. Like the Mothers of the *Plaza de Mayo*, Antígona resents being hindered in what she perceives to be her role as woman. Her love for Hemón and her love for Polinices are made impossible by Creonte's tyranny, which leads her to actions that question the national concept put forth by Creonte and the *Corifeo*. The national community imagined by the tyrant excludes women. In this context, it is significant that Gambaro chose Antinoo as the *Corifeo's* partner and audience. Antinoo (Antinoüs) was Roman emperor Hadrian's lover, and, after his accidental death, became a much worshipped symbol of male beauty. The bond between the Corifeo and Antinoo thus is an allegory for a state based on masculine hegemony, and exclusive of things female. Antígona's traditional role as nurturer and caretaker who refuses to remain marginal, becomes subversive when wielded as a weapon. For Antígona, born to love, and not to hate in the name of the "national brotherhood," the *Corifeo's* words hold no meaning: "Despicable are those who hold a loved one in higher esteem than their own fatherland" (p. 202). *Patria*, "fatherland," remains an abstract entity, a mirror that does not reflect women.

Staged for an Argentine audience, the universal parable of the tragic fate of the woman who stood up against her government in order to fulfill what she perceived to be her sisterly duties, contains a concrete and obvious testimony to the courage of the *locas* of the Plaza de Mayo, and a warning against the loss of memory.

Theatre—often a looking glass for society's flaws—in Gambaro's case, as in that of many Argentine playwrights, is not only a highly developed art form, but also an instrument of unceasing criticism of the socio-political context. Like her male colleagues (Dragún, Pavlovsky, Jorge Goldenberg, to name just a few), she is interested in creating theatre for social change. The portrayal of the ruthlessness of the authoritarian regime and the condemnation of individual passivity in the struggle against the former are the central themes in her theatre. For Gambaro, her political commitment has gradually raised questions about the role of women in the struggle for equal distribution of power in Argentine society. This is reflected in the increasing number of women protagonists in her plays, and the association of resistance against oppression with a rebellious female character set against a dictatorial male. During the years of the worst repression (1976-1983), the world of politics—once, according to Gambaro, "the world of men, the political world"—ceased to be an exclusively male domain. Circumstances forced women out of their homes to protest the repression. Gambaro, herself from a working class background, seems to have followed a path similar to that of the *Madres*, whose participation in politics has spurred a lively debate on the place of women in society (Rossi).

Gambaro's theatre is testimony to the fact that even in democracy there is room and demand for politically conscious theatre. As Antígona says, there is not yet room for love or, in other words, for strictly personal concerns. Women's rights, exercised independently of political issues of more general interest, are not yet a priority. However, through her increasing interest in strong female protagonists, particularly in her plays after 1983, Gambaro seems to indicate that the time has come to include the specific concerns of women in the political (democratic) agenda. Gambaro ties her development of a feminist discourse to the emancipation of the community as a whole, stressing the potentially powerful qualities inherent in women's traditional gender role. Her female protagonists operate as symbols of hope and freedom, projecting images of the nurturing love of a mother (Suki) or the devotion of a sister (Antígona). The metaphorization of women (compare Suki, metaphorical presentation of the subjected Argentina) may be regarded as the integration of a political with a potentially feminist discourse. This phenomenon, which does not occur in such an obvious fashion among the more personally focused Spanish playwrights, places Gambaro's theatre firmly in the Latin American context. However, despite the justified criticism that the excessive emphasis on the sociopolitical element of Latin American art forms sometimes sparks (Barnard, "Popular Cinema" 60), in the case of the playwrights discussed here, this emphasis seems to be enlightening, relevant, and appropriate.

The course of Argentina's political and economic development since 1930, is mirrored in the theatre of this country. It is not surprising that even playwrights increasingly concerned with so-called "subjective" themes, like women's role in society, still give priority to the critical surveillance of a political system that, at any moment, might collapse and be replaced by another dictatorship.

More than their Spanish colleagues, Bortnik and Gambaro have analyzed their country's political scene and have made the individual responsible for political change, even though from completely different perspectives, and governed by their different styles. One might call Gambaro's theatre more stylized, more concentrated on the one central theme of the relationship between victim and oppressor. Bortnik prefers the presentation of almost *costumbrista* detail, of personal lives and relationships viewed against the background of a frightening and frustrating political reality that, despite her reference to concrete facts, seems at times almost remote when compared to the gruesome atmosphere of repression in Gambaro's theatre. Despite these differences, both playwrights coincide in underlining each individual's personal responsibility in the process of social and political change. Both tie together politics and women's issues, although neither has (yet) developed a coherent feminist discourse. While in the case of Gambaro one may speak of the unhalting development of a feminist perspective, Bortnik's work wavers between the expression of feminist concerns (criticism of the role of the housewife in *Domesticados*, and of violence against women in *La isla*), and the portrayal of women following traditional role

models.   The surprising contrast between the bitter Ana
(*Domesticados*), or the increasingly independent, knowledge-
seeking Alicia (*La historia oficial*) on the one hand, and the
nurturing, selfless, and sometimes fragile women in *Primaveras* or
in *La isla* on the other hand, underscores the difficulty of shaping
a feminist discourse in a genre where the modes of expression
and production have been traditionally male dominated.

However, traditional female roles may contain the seeds of
revolution. Particularly in the work written after the democratic
transition, Bortnik and Gambaro emphasize the role of women in
political change. Although the female protagonists often become
politically conscious and rebellious through the fate of their male
kin rather than feminist consciousness (Antígona through the fate
of her brother's body, Alicia through her adoptive daughter), the
stories of their emancipation show that women cannot be
marginal to politics. The term "politics," after all, comes from the
Greek *politikos*, "citizen," which today comprises female as well as
male. Repression, as Argentina's recent history has shown, does
not stop at the doors of the private household. Indeed, it starts in
the heart of the family, with the relationship between husband
and wife. Bortnik's and Gambaro's work reflects a reality where
women, forced by circumstance, leave the domestic realm to
prove that their actions and opinions do count, that they can
succeed where their male partners have failed.   Interestingly
enough, both playwrights pit strong, questioning women against
an overwhelmingly male, repressive system (*Del sol naciente*,
Antígona furiosa, *La historia oficial*). Theirs is a path to self-reliance
and independence through politics, an experience not shared by
the Spanish women dramatists.   As democracy stabilizes in
Argentina,   and   the   disillusionment   over   the   negligible
participation of women in the political arena further increases
(Walsh), we may see a development of theatre by women
playwrights similar to the one in Spain. The next generation of
women playwrights may turn to more personal themes, like the
discussion of domestic issues, interpersonal relationships, and
personal creativity. Looking at the sociopolitical committment of
Argentine women playwrights today, however, there seems to be
little possibility for theatre solely as "a place for amusement."

Notes

[1]This "radical devaluation of language" Martin Esslin observes in the theatre of the absurd: ". . . what happens on the stage transcends, and often contradicts, the words spoken by the characters" (p. 7).

[2]See plays like Samuel Beckett's *Waiting for Godot* and *Endgame*.

[3]See Stella Maris-Martini, Teresa Méndez-Faith, Lucía Lockert, et al.

[4]Gambaro, "¿Es posible y deseable una dramaturgia específicamente femenina?" p. 21.

[5]Gambaro's unveiled accusation of the repression in Argentina during the years of the *guerra sucia* [the "dirty war"] in *Información para extranjeros* (1974) endangered her and her family's lives (Interview with Betsko and Koenig, p. 187)

[6]On language and power see also Méndez-Faith, "Sobre el uso y abuso del poder en la producción dramática de Griselda Gambaro."

[7]See Podol's excellent comparative study of Spanish playwright Buero Vallejo's *La fundación* (1974) and *Las paredes*, "Reality Perception and Stage Setting . . . "

[8]Compare the death of the protagonist in Discépolo's play *Stéfano*, where the loss of the character's ability to speak or to move reflects his inability to communicate with an alienating environment.

Conclusions

The scantily clad woman whose head is split open for inspection and manipulation by a member of the armed forces on the cover of Varela-Cid and Vicens's book *La imbecilización de la mujer* speaks of the patriarchal control to which women have been traditionally subjected under dictatorial military governments. Both in Spain and Argentina, repressive leadership created a climate not conducive to women's participation in public life. While this situation has changed as a result of democratic transformations during the last two decades, a great deal remains to be done in terms of the recognition of women's contributions in areas of traditionally male domain.

The purpose of this book has been the analysis of the work of representative women playwrights in Spain and Argentina, in the light of recent sociopolitical changes. As I had assumed, their presence or absence from the stage, and the form and content of their theatre, has been closely linked to their social and political environment. While I do not want to overemphasize the relationship between theatre and politics, being aware of the dangers such an approach may entail, I believe the discussion of the historical background is essential for the fair and thorough appraisal of this theatre's significance. Indeed, the playwrights dealt with in this study are openly committed to social change, be it in the more general terms of political progress and social justice, or in the more concrete terms of the rights of women. Their theatre is therefore directly responsive to its sociopolitical environment.

The political transition from dictatorship to democracy in both countries has had a dramatic effect on the work of women playwrights. In Spain, their number has increased considerably in the past ten years. For the first time in three decades, after a long, almost complete absence from the stage, we are again able to speak of a generation of women dramatists. Themes seldom or never discussed in public by women under the dictatorship of General Francisco Franco, often become the central focus in the plays of Carmen Resino, Pilar Pombo, Maribel Lázaro, and Paloma Pedrero. Dissatisfaction with traditional female role-playing is expressed in almost all of Pedrero's plays, but particularly in *Besos de lobo* (1987), *La noche dividida* (1989), and *El color de agosto* (1988). The problematic search for the identity of the woman artist is the subject of *El color de agosto* and of Pombo's *Una comedia de encargo* (1988). Problems of sexual identity are addressed in Pedrero's *La llamada de Lauren* (1985) and in *El color de agosto*, and also in Pombo's *Una comedia de encargo*, and in Lázaro's *La fuga* (1986).

While these playwrights do not have a particularly rich tradition of women dramatists to look back upon, they are not completely alone in Spanish theatre history. The successful playwrighting of Ana Diosdado bridges the wide gap between the stoutly conservative, pro-Franco generation of the forties and fifties (María Isabel Suárez de Deza, Mercedes Ballesteros, etc.), and the young dramatists of the eighties. The progressive gloss-over of Diosdado's theatre is indicative of the changes that were operating in Spanish society in the seventies and early eighties, and in some ways foreshadows the preoccupations of a Pedrero or a Pombo. However, her ultimately conservative viewpoints, particularly regarding male-female relationships and women's roles, place Diosdado among the women dramatists of the Franco era. Her plays deal with a variety of themes: the meaninglessness of ideologies in *Olvida los tambores* (1970), the exploitation of the individual in a consumer society in *Usted también puede disfrutar de ella* (1973), and the importance of love and family in a woman's life in *Anillos de oro* (1983) and in *Camino de plata* (1988). While the conflicts in Diosdado's plays are often resolved in a traditional fashion—love, understanding, and even marriage being common solutions—Pedrero's theatre usually ends in separation rather than union. For Pedrero and several in her generation, the individual, and particularly the woman, ultimately is alone, all ties to previously valid and powerful institutions severed. The loss of the defining and confining community (family, marriage, friends) has left a field of ruins where the female protagonist has to pick up the pieces in order to create a new identity.

In Argentina, the presence of women dramatists—not, however, the form and content of their work—seems less dependent on political change. Griselda Gambaro and Aída Bortnik (together with Roma Mahieu, Hebe Serebrisky, and others) have been writing since the sixties and early seventies, and have continued to do so in spite of persecution and exile under the *proceso* governments (1976-1983). In addition, the democratic transition (1983) has not silenced their voices of dissent. Like other Argentine women dramatists (Mahieu, Fernández Tiscornia), they believe in the social responsibility of the playwright, and are both therefore highly political. Gambaro deals mostly with the relationship of dependency between victim and oppressor in a dictatorial society, and the dangers of individual passivity in the face of repression. Bortnik focuses on the loss of idealism in Western society and the frustration the betrayal of one's beliefs engenders. Both dramatists coincide in their emphasis on the individual's responsibility for social and political change.

For Gambaro and Bortnik the political opening has meant not so much a complete change of subject matter, as a shift of focus; their more recent work includes issues previously neglected. Gambaro's writing has developed from displaying a predominantly male perspective on matters of sociopolitical interest to a more woman-centered and sometimes even feminist position. In her first plays both victim and oppressor are male and women characters are absent (*Las paredes* [1963]), or women characters are patterned after traditional female roles (*El desatino* [1965], *Dar la vuelta* [1973]). In her later plays, the victim and rebel-to-be is a woman. In *El despojamiento* (1974), Gambaro questions the role-playing a woman is forced to do in a society that regards her as object rather than individual. In *Del sol naciente* (1984) and *Antígona furiosa* (1986), the female protagonist rebels against the cruelty and arbitrariness of (male) dictatorial power, without, however, completely relinquishing traditional female roles.

Like Gambaro, Bortnik in her theatre and scriptwriting emphasizes the impossibility of a separation between the personal and the public. *Domesticados* (1982), *Primaveras* (1984), and *La historia oficial* (1985) underline that political change or stagnation are projections and consequences of individual participation or passivity. However, Bortnik's search for social justice and political progress has not consistently embraced a preoccupation with women's issues. Her discourse wavers between a thoroughly male point of view, that reserves certain traditional feminine roles for the women characters (*La isla* [1976], *Primaveras*), and a feminist critique of the duties and responsibilities assigned to women in patriarchal culture (*Domesticados*, *La historia oficial*).

While I did expect to see a shift in the focus of women's playwrighting after the democratic transitions, I was suprised at how different the overall response of the Argentine playwrights was from that of the Spaniards. At first sight, a superficially similar political development might be expected to generate similar preoccupations in the work of committed playwrights. I expected this particularly since the dramatists discussed here share the experience of being a minority in a male-dominated genre and of being engaged opinion-holders in a society that only reluctantly values women's utterances. In Argentina, Gambaro and Bortnik are outspokenly committed to engaged playwriting. Both believe in the social responsibility of the writer. During the years of the harshest dictatorship, they formed, together with other playwrights, one of the last havens of encumbered, but nevertheless existing, dissent. During the nineteen eighties, worried about the future of a fragile democracy in their country, they continued to wield a politically critical pen. In keeping with the dominant trend of Latin American feminism, they tend not to separate feminist preoccupations from broader political concerns. Only gradually, and parallel to the political opening, have they focussed on the development of a feminist discourse, which still remains secondary to a more general political critique.

While the motivation behind much of the theatre written by Spain's newest women playwrights may be considered political, it would be wrong to apply this term to their work. Coming back to Kirby's definition, political theatre is "intentionally engaged or consciously takes sides in politics." This is generally not the case in the plays of Pedrero or Pombo. The absence of political commitment in theatre by Spanish women dramatists has a long tradition. The handful of women playwrights who saw their work staged during the forties and fifties conformed to conservative patterns of female conduct. One could apply Jacques Ellul's term "propaganda of integration" to these playwrights' open commitment to Franquista ideals of Catholic womanhood and patriarchal culture. Theatre, like that of Gambaro in Argentina, containing "propaganda of agitation," which "can be understood as a call for action" and challenges existing political power structures, cannot, as a rule, be found in Spain (Foulkes 11). Diosdado occasionally refers to the political and social transformations happening in Spain during the late seventies. However, her plays are tinged with nostalgia for the Spain left behind. In spite of the potential critical value her theatre might have, it is ultimately conservative and differs vastly from the work her Argentine colleagues have written in times of dictatorship.

The absence of political themes in the theatre of the young dramatists of the eighties can be explained in part by their lack of experience with dictatorship. Spain's democracy is now almost two decades old and fairly healthy compared to the fledgling young democracy in Argentina. Although according to Buero-Vallejo "there continue being problems of a political or social order that could merit criticism from the stage," these are not as urgent as they were under Franco's regime (Personal interview). Nevertheless, the work of several of the young women dramatists of the eighties is far from what Fortes calls "literatura light" or from the escapist trends Moxon-Browne observed in Spanish democratic culture. While their commitment is rather more social than political, and their criticism focuses on women's issues rather than broader political questions, their approach to theatre is in essence the same as Gambaro's or Bortnik's: They regard theatre as a critical mirror of society and as a tool for social change.

The reasons behind the difference in focus of the plays by the Argentine and the Spanish women dramatists analyzed here are manifold. It seems safe to assume that the diverse make-up of Argentine society, a fairly prominent early feminist movement, and governments more or less sympathetic to the rights of women (Sarmiento, Perón) made a certain political self-confidence among women possible in Argentina. It is also important to keep in mind the incredible brutality of the *proceso* governments whose repression reached deep into the heart of the Argentine family, thus forcing women to become political, even if it was to defend their roles as wives and mothers rather than to rally for the feminist cause. In Spain, a long history of women's oppression and forty years of Francoist propaganda effectively silenced women. A political system that despite its repressive tactics lacked the harrowing brutality of the *proceso* regime, seems to have been more successful than the latter in engendering passivity concerning political matters.

The separation of politics and feminism in the work of Spanish women dramatists, and the priority politics have over feminist preoccupations in the work of the Argentine women playwrights, have led to two different kinds of theatre. Pedrero's plays can be considered feminist according to Janet Brown's definition: "If the agent is a woman, her purpose autonomy, and the scene an unjust socio-sexual hierarchy, the play is a feminist drama" (16). All of the plays discussed in this study, however, show elements of what Shulamith Firestone calls a theatre of "androgenous mentality." This type of theatre, rather than describing situations free of gender conflict, is testimony to the ongoing struggle between sexual and human identity (Register 6).

Democratic transition in Argentina has moved the concern with gender-based social problems more toward the center of attention, and has thus brought the Argentine playwrights closer to their Spanish colleagues in terms of the themes addressed in their work. The success of the four dramatists studied here in beginning to fashion a feminist discourse in a language and a genre shaped by patriarchy, may help dispel the notion that there is no room in modern democratic societies for a theatre that takes sides.

Bibliography

Archenti, Nélida. *Situación de la mujer en la sociedad argentina: formas de organización en la Capital Federal*. Buenos Aires: Fundación Friedrich Naumann, 1987.

Atwood, Margaret. *Cat's Eye*. Toronto: McClelland and Stewart, 1988.

Avellaneda, Andrés. *Censura, autoritarismo y cultura: Argentina 1960 1983*. 2 vols. Buenos Aires: Centro Editor de América Latina, 1986.

_____. "Argentina militar: los discursos del silencio." *Literatura argentina de hoy: De la dictadura a la democracia*. Editors Karl Kohut and Andrea Pagni. Frankfurt: Vervuert, 1989. 13–30.

Ballesteros, Mercedes, Claudio de la Torre. *Quiero ver al doctor*. Madrid: Ediciones Alfil, 1953.

Barnard, Tim. "Popular Cinema and Populist Politics." *Argentine Cinema*. Ed. Barnard. Toronto: Brightwood Editions, 1986. 5–63.

Barrios de Chungara, Domitila. *Wenn man mir erlaubt zu sprechen*. Trans. Carmen Alicia Egas de Boll and René Boll-Muta. Ed. Moema Viezzer. Bornheim–Merten: Verlag Lamuv, 1978.

Beckett, Samuel. *Waiting for Godot*. New York: Grove Press, 1954.

Belsey, Catherine, Jane Moore, eds. *The Feminist Reader: Essays in Gender and the Politics of Literary Criticism*. New York: Blackwell, 1989.

Beltrán, Nuria. *¿Muerte civil de la española?* Barcelona: Plaza y Janés, 1975.

Bentley, Eric. "Writing for a Political Theatre." *Performing Arts Journal* 11.26/27 (1985): 45–59.

Berger, John. *Ways of Seeing*. London: Penguin, 1977.

Bergmann, Emilie, et al. *Women, Culture, and Politics in Latin America*. Seminar on Feminism and Culture in Latin America. Berkeley: University of California Press, 1990.

Betsko, Kathleen, and Rachel Koenig. *Interviews with Contemporary Women Playwrights*. New York: Beech Tree Books, 1987.

Blanco Amores de Pagella, Angela. *Motivaciones del teatro argentino en el siglo XX*. Buenos Aires: Ediciones Culturales Argentinas, 1983.

Boling, Becky. "From Pin-Ups to Striptease in Gambaro's *El despojamiento*." *Latin American Theatre Review* 20.2 (Spring 1987): 59–65.

Bonafini, Hebe de. Interview. "Mis hijos me parieron a mí." *Alfonsina* 1.4 (January 1984): 4–5.

_____. "No vamos a claudicar." *Madres de Plaza de Mayo* 1.1 (December 1984): 2

Bortnik, Aída. *La isla*. Ed. Jorge Miguel Couselo. Buenos Aires: Centro Editor de América Latina, 1981.

_____. *Papá querido. Teatro breve contemporáneo argentino*. Eds. Elvira Burlando de Meyer and Patricio Esteve. Buenos Aires: Ediciones Colihue, 1981.

_____. Interview. *Primaveras*. 9–24.

_____. *Primaveras*. Buenos Aires: Teatro Municipal General San Martín, 1985.

_____. *Domesticados*. Buenos Aires: Argentores, 1988.

_____. "Participar desde lo propio." *La participación política de la mujer: Encuentro nacional*. Buenos Aires: Fundación Centro de Participación Política, 1988. 56–60.

_____, and Luis Puenzo. *La historia oficial.* Buenos Aires: Ediciones de la Urraca, 1985.

Brown, Janet. *Feminist Drama: Definition and Critical Analysis.* Metuchen, NJ: Scarecrow P, 1979.

Buero Vallejo, Antonio. Personal interview. May 31, 1989.

Bunster-Burotto, Ximena. "Surviving Beyond Fear: Women and Torture in Latin America." *Women and Change in Latin America.* Eds. June Nash and Helen Safa. South Hadley, MA: Bergin and Garvey Publishers, 1986. 297–325.

Capmany, Maria Aurelia. *El feminismo ibérico.* Barcelona: Oikos-tan ediciones, 1970.

Carlson, Marifran. *¡Feminismo!: The Women's Movement in Argentina: From Its Beginnings to Eva Perón.* Chicago: Academy, 1988.

Casas, Nelly. *Compromiso ser mujer.* Buenos Aires: Peña Lillo Editor, 1985.

Cassaux, Manuel P. "La censura y otros demonios." *Primer Acto* 184 (April–May 1980): 90–91.

Caudet, Francisco. *Crónica de una marginación: Conversaciones con Alfonso Sastre.* Madrid: Ediciones de la Torre, 1984.

Cosentino, Olga. "1984–1987: La democracia, un avance lento e inseguro." *Escenarios de dos mundos.* 4 vols. Madrid: Centro de Documentación Teatral, 1988. Vol. 1: 152–57.

Couselo, Jorge Miguel. Preface. Aída Bortnik. *La isla.* i–vii.

Cypess, Sandra Messinger. "The Plays of Griselda Gambaro." *Dramatists in Revolt: The New Latin American Theatre.* Eds. Leon F. Lyday and George Woodyard. Austin: U of Texas P, 1976. 95–109.

Dahlerup, Drude. *The New Women's Movement.* London: Sage, 1986.

Damian, Michael. *Zur Geschichtlichkeit des Theaters des Absurden.* Frankfurt: Haag und Herchen, 1977.

Diosdado, Ana. *Olvida los tambores. Teatro español 1970–1971.* Editor F. C. Sainz de Robles. Madrid: Aguilar, 1972.

_____. *El okapi.* Madrid: Escelicer, 1972.

_____. *Usted también podrá disfrutar de ella. Teatro español 1973–1974.* Ed. F. C. Sainz de Robles. Madrid: Aguilar, 1975.

_____. *Anillos de oro.* 2 vols. Madrid: Espasa-Calpe, 1985.

_____. *Cuplé.* Madrid: Ediciones Antonio Machado, 1988.

_____. *Los ochenta son nuestros.* Madrid: Ediciones MK, 1988.

_____. *Camino de plata.* Madrid: Ediciones Antonio Machado, 1990.

Discépolo, Armando. *Mateo. Stéfano. Relojero.* Ed. Luis Ordaz. Buenos Aires: Centro Editor de América Latina, 1980.

Dragún, Osvaldo. "Teatro, creación y realidad latinoamericana." *Hoy_se comen al flaco. Al violador.* Ottawa: Girol Books, 1981. 7–38.

Ellmann, Mary. *Thinking About Women.* New York: Harcourt, Brace and World, 1968.

España, Claudio. "Sugerir en función de la escritura." *La historia oficial.* 3–5.

Esslin, Martin. *The Theatre of the Absurd.* New York: Doubleday, 1969.

Fabj, Valeria. "Motherhood as Political Voice: The Rhetoric of the Mothers of Plaza de Mayo." *Communication Studies* 44 (Spring 1993): 1–18.

Facio, Angel, et al. "Mesa Redonda de actores." *Primer Acto* 184 (April–May 1980): 105–115.

Fagundo, Ana María. "El teatro de Ana Diosdado." *Alaluz* 18.2 (1986): 51–59.

Falcón, Lidia. *No moleste, calle y pague, señora. Dramaturgas españolas de hoy: Una introducción.* Ed. Patricia O'Connor. Madrid: Fundamentos, 1988.

Feijoó, María del Carmen. "The Challenge of Constructing Civilian Peace: Women and Democracy in Argentina." *The Women's Movement in Latin America: Feminism and the Transition to Democracy.* Ed. Jane S. Jaquette. Boston: Unwin Hyman, 1989. 72–94.

_____, and Elizabeth Jelin. "Después del decenio, ¿qué?" *Debate* 3 (April–May 1985): 37.

_____, and Elizabeth Jelin. "España: Feminismo y política." *Debate* 2 (Sept.–Oct. 1984): 43.

Felski, Rita. *Beyond Feminist Aesthetics: Feminist Literature and Social Change.* Cambridge: Harvard U P, 1989.

Féral, Josette. "Writing and Displacement: Women in Theatre." *Modern Drama* 27.4 (1984): 549–61.

Fernández, Gerardo. "1949–1983: Del peronismo a la dictadura militar." *Escenarios de dos mundos.* 4 vols. Madrid: Centro de Documentación Teatral, 1988. Vol 1: 135–51.

_____. "El país de los dramaturgos." *El Periodista* 235, 24 Mar. 1989: 38–40.

Figes, Eva. *Patriarchal Attitudes: Women in Society.* New York: Stein and Day, 1970.

154

Fisher, Jo. *Mothers of the Disappeared*. Boston: South End P, 1989.

Fortes, José Antonio. *Novelas para la transición política*. Madrid: Ediciones Libertarias, 1987.

Foulkes, A. P. *Literature and Propaganda*. London: Methuen, 1983.

Franco, Jean. "Self-Destructing Heroines." *The Minnesota Review* 22 (Spring 1984): 105–15.

Friedan, Betty. *The Feminine Mystique*. New York: Dell, 1964.

Fuentes Mares, José. *La joven Antígona se va a la guerra*. *Teatro*. México: Editorial Jus, 1969.

Gambaro, Griselda. *Teatro*. Vols. 1–4. Buenos Aires: Ediciones de la Flor, 1984–1990.

_____. *Las paredes. El desatino*. *Teatro*. Vol. 4. Buenos Aires: Ediciones de la Flor, 1990.

_____. *Dar la vuelta. Información para extranjeros*. *Teatro*. Vol. 2. Buenos Aires: Ediciones de la Flor, 1987.

_____. *La malasangre. Del sol naciente*. *Teatro*. Vol. 1. Buenos Aires: Ediciones de la Flor, 1984.

_____. *La gracia. Decir sí. El despojamiento. Antígona furiosa*. *Teatro*. Vol. 3. Buenos Aires: Ediciones de la Flor, 1989.

_____. *Nada que ver. Sucede lo que pasa*. Eds. Miguel Angel Giella, Peter Roster, Leandro Urbina. Ottawa: Girol Books, 1983.

_____. "¿Es posible y deseable una dramaturgia específicamente femenina?" *Latin American Theatre Review* 13.2 (1980): 17–22.

_____. Interview. "La ética de la confrontación." *Nada que ver* 7–20.

_____. Interview. "La difícil perfección." *Nada que ver* 21–37.

_____. *Lo impenetrable*. Buenos Aires: Torres Agüero, 1984.

_____. "Algunas consideraciones sobre la mujer y la literatura." *Revista Iberoamericana* 51.132–33 (1985): 471–73.

_____. Interview. *Women's Voices From Latin America*. Ed. Evelyn Picon-Garfield. Detroit: Wayne State U P, 1985. 53–72.

_____. Interview. "Griselda Gambaro habla de su obra más reciente y la crítica." Sharon Magnarelli. *Revista de Estudios Hispánicos* 20.1 (Jan. 1986): 123–33.

_____. Interview. *Interviews with Contemporary Women Playwrights*. Eds. Kathleen Betsko and Rachel Koenig. New York: Beech Tree Books, 1987. 184–99.

_____, Sara Facio, et al. "Feminismo y democracia: mujeres con el pelo corto y las ideas largas." *El Periodista* 33, 26 April 1985: 43–45.

García Lorenzo, Luciano, and Francisca Vilches de Frutos. *La temporada teatral española 1983–1984*. Madrid: Anejos de la Revista Segismundo, 1985.

Garfield, Evelyn. *Women's Voices from Latin America*. Detroit: Wayne State U P. 1985.

Garrido, José Manuel. Interview with Antonio Núñez. *Insula* (Nov–Dec 1984).

Gerdes, Dick. "Recent Argentine Vanguard Theatre: Gambaro's *Información para extranjeros*." *Latin American Theatre Review* 11.2 (Spring 1978): 11–16.

Graham-Yooll, Andrew. *A State of Fear: Memories of Argentina's Nightmare*. London: Eland, 1986.

Hadas, Moses, ed. *Greek Drama*. New York: Bantam Books, 1971.

Halsey, Martha, and Phyllis Zatlin. "Is There Life After Lorca?" *The Contemporary Spanish Theater: A Collection of Critical Essays.*

156

Eds. Halsey and Zatlin. Lanham, MD: U P of America, 1988. 1–24.

Holzapfel, Tamara. "Griselda Gambaro's Theatre of the Absurd." *Latin_American Theatre Review* 4.1 (Fall 1970): 5–11.

Hormigón, Juan Antonio. "Luces y sombras del presente teatral." *El_Público* 6 (June 1984): 3–5.

Hutcheon, Linda. *A Poetics of Postmodernism*. New York: Routledge, 1988.

Jaquette, Jane S, Ed. *The Women's Movement in Latin America: Feminism and the Transition to Democracy*. Boston: Unwyn Hyman, 1989.

Kaiser-Lenoir, Claudia. *El grotesco criollo: Estilo teatral de una época*. La Habana: Casa de las Américas, 1977.

Kafka, Franz. *La metamorfosis*. Trans. Jorge Luis Borges. Valencia: Círculo de Lectores, 1986.

Kirby, Michael. "On Political Theatre." *The Drama Review* 19.2 (June 1975): 129–35.

Kiss, Marilyn Frances. *The Labyrinth of Cruelty: A Study of Selected Works of Griselda Gambaro*. Diss. Rutgers University, 1982. Ann Arbor: UMI, 1982. 8221683.

Kohut, Karl, and Andrea Pagni, eds. *Literatura argentina de hoy: De la dictadura a la democracia*. Frankfurt: Vervuert, 1989.

Kristeva, Julia. "Women's Time." Belsey and Moore 197–218.

Laughlin, Karen L. "The Language of Cruelty: Dialogue Strategies and the Spectator in Gambaro's *El desatino* and Pinter's *The Birthday Party*." *Latin American Theatre Review* 20.1 (Fall 1986): 11–20.

Lewald, H. Ernest. "Two Generations of River Plate Women Writers." *Latin American Research Review* 5.1 (1980): 231–35.

Lockert, Lucía. "Aggression and Submission in Griselda Gambaro's *The_Walls*." *Michigan Academician* 19.1 (Winter 1987): 37–42.

López Negrín, Florentino. "El tedio inacabable." *El Independiente* (Summer 1990): 30.

Maris-Martini, Stella. "La 'Comedia Humana' según Gambaro." *Poder, deseo y marginación: Aproximaciones a la obra de Griselda Gambaro*. Ed. Nora Mazziotti. Buenos Aires: Punto Sur Editores, 1989. 25–40.

Martin, Alfredo. *Les Mères "folles" de la Place de Mai*. Paris: Renaudot et Cie, 1989.

Martín, Sabas. "Joven teatro español." *Cuadernos Hispanoamericanos* 466 (1989): 171–79.

Martínez, Martha. "Tres dramaturgas argentinas: Roma Mahieu, Hebe Urhart y Diana Raznovich." *Latin American Theatre Review* 13.2 (Spring 1980): 39–45.

Mátar, Beatriz. Interview. Bortnik. *Primaveras*. 25–28.

Mazziotti, Nora, ed. *Poder, deseo y marginación: Aproximaciones a la obra de Griselda Gambaro*. Buenos Aires: Punto Sur Editores, 1989.

Méndez-Faith, Teresa. "Sobre el uso y abuso de poder en la producción dramática de Griselda Gambaro." *Revista Iberoamericana* 51 (Jul.–Dec. 1985): 831–41.

Modleski, Tania. *Loving with a Vengeance: Mass-produced Fantasies for Women*. New York: Routledge, 1988.

Moi, Toril. "Feminist, Female, Feminine." Belsey and Moore 117–32.

Moxon-Browne, Edward. *Political Change in Spain*. London: Routledge, 1989.

158

O'Connor, Patricia. "Spain's First Successful Woman Dramatist: María Martínez Sierra." *Hispanófila* 66 (1978): 87–108.

_____. "¿Quiénes son las dramaturgas españolas y qué han escrito?" *Estreno* 10.2 (1984): 9–12.

_____. "Las dramaturgas españolas y la otra censura." *Diálogos hispánicos de Amsterdam: Censura y literatura peninsulares.* Amsterdam: Rodopi, 1987. 99–117.

_____. "A Theater in Transition: From Paternalism to Pornography." Halsey and Zatlin 201–13.

_____. *Dramaturgas españolas de hoy: una introducción.* Madrid: Fundamentos, 1988.

_____. "Six *Dramaturgas* in Search of a Stage." *Gestos* 5 (1988): 116–20.

Oliva, César. *El teatro desde 1936.* Madrid Alhambra, 1989.

Oliva, María Victoria. "El espaldarazo de Tirso." *El Público* 52 (1988): 41.

Ortiz, Lourdes, et al. "Nuevas autoras: Coloquio." *Primer Acto* 220 (1987): 11–21.

Parsons, Robert. "Reversals of Illocutionary Logic in Griselda Gambaro's *Las paredes.*" *Things Done With Words: Speech Acts in Hispanic Drama.* Ed. Elias Rivers. Newark: Juan de la Cuesta, 1986. 101–14.

Pavlovsky, Eduardo. Preface. *Potestad.* Buenos Aires: Búsqueda, 1987. 13–17.

Pedrero, Paloma. *La llamada de Lauren.* Madrid: Ediciones Antonio Machado, 1987.

_____. *Besos de lobo. Invierno de luna alegre.* Madrid: Editorial Fundamentos, 1987.

_____. *Resguardo personal*. *Dramaturgas españolas de hoy*. Ed. Patricia O'Connor. Madrid: Fundamentos, 1988.

_____. *El color de agosto*. *La noche dividida*. Madrid: Ediciones Antonio Machado, 1989.

_____. *Noches de amor efímero*. Murcia: Universidad de Murcia, 1991.

Pérez, Janet. *Contemporary Women Writers of Spain*. Boston: Twayne Publishers, 1988.

Piglia, Ricardo. "Ficción y política en la literatura argentina." Kohut and Pagni 97–104.

Población, Félix. "La Compañía Argentina con dos autores de hoy." *El Público* 32 (May 1986): 48–51.

Podol, Peter. "Reality Perception and Stage Setting in Griselda Gambaro's *Las paredes* and Antonio Buero Vallejo's *La fundación*." *Modern Drama* 24.1 (March 1981): 44–53.

Poe, Edgar Allan. *Collected Works*. 3 vols. Ed. Thomas Ollive Mabbot. Cambridge: Belknap Press, 1969.

Pombo, Pilar. *Una comedia de encargo*. Madrid: n. p., 1984. (Colección La Comedia).

_____. *Amalia*. Madrid: n.p., 1986.

_____. *Isabel*. Madrid: n.p., 1987.

_____. *Purificación*. Madrid: n.p., 1987.

_____. *Remedios*. *Dramaturgas españolas de hoy*. Ed. Patricia O'Connor. Madrid: Fundamentos, 1988.

"¿Por qué no estrenan las mujeres en España? (Encuesta)." *Estreno* 10.2 (1984): 13–25.

Postma, Rosalea. "Space and Spectator in the Theatre of Griselda Gambaro: *Información para extranjeros.*" *Latin American Theatre Review* 14.1 (Fall 1980): 35–45.

Prates, Suzana. "Women's Work in the Southern Cone: Monetarist Policies in Argentina, Uruguay and Chile." *Latin American Women.* Ed. Olivia Harris. London: Minority Rights Group Report 57, March 1983. 10.

Pratt, Mary Louise. "Women, Literature, and National Brotherhood." Bergmann et al. 48–73.

Pross, Edith. "Open Theatre Revisited: An Argentine Experiment." *Latin American Theatre Review* 18.1 (Fall 1984): 83–94.

Register, Cheri. "American Feminist Criticism: A Bibliographical Introduction." *Feminist Literary Criticism: Explorations in Theory.* Ed. Josephine Donovan. Kentucky: The U P of Kentucky, 1975. 1–28.

Resino, Carmen. *Nueva historia de la princesa y el dragón.* Madrid: Editorial Lucerna, 1989.

_____. *Teatro breve y El oculto enemigo del profesor Schneider.* Madrid: Fundamentos, 1990.

Rock, David. *Argentina 1516–1987: From Spanish Colonization to Alfonsín.* Berkeley: U of California P, 1987.

Rossi, Laura. "Una nueva relación entre ética y política." *Madres de Plaza de Mayo* 4.41 (May 1988): 15–16.

Roster, Peter. "'Lo grotesco,' 'El Grotesco Criollo' y la obra dramática de Griselda Gambaro." Mazziotti 55–63.

Salas, Horacio. "Radio y televisión en la transición democrática." Kohut and Pagni 67–75.

Salvat, Ricard. "Teatro de autor." *Boletín Informativo Fundación Juan March* 194 (1989).

Sánchez, Luis Rafael. *La pasión según Antígona Pérez*. Barcelona: Ediciones Lugar, 1970.

Sangüesa, Agustina. "Paloma Pedrero: El realismo marginal de un sueño." *El Público* 66 (1989): 28–30.

Santa-Cruz, Lola. "*Cuplé*: Ana Diosdado, inteligencia al servicio de la coherencia." *El Público* 39 (1986): 28–30.

Sastre. Alfonso. "Mis críticas al franquismo se subvencionan, las actuales no." *El Independiente* Jan. 17, 1990: 30.

Scott-Kinzer, Nora. "Sexist Sociology." *The Center Magazine* (May–Jun. 1974): 48–60.

Sontag, Susan. "Theater and Film." *Film and/as Literature*. Editor John Harrington. Englewood Cliffs, New Jersey: Prentice Hall, 1977. 76–92.

Sophocles. *Antigone. Greek Drama*. Ed. Moses Hadas. New York: Bantam Books, 1971.

Staiff, Kive. "Los empeños del Teatro San Martín." *El Público* 61 (Oct 1988): 17–19.

Suárez de Deza, Isabel. *Buenas noches*. Madrid: Ediciones Alfil, 1952.

Szanto, George. *Theatre and Propaganda*. Austin: U of Texas P, 1978.

Threlfall, Monica. "The Women's Movement in Spain." *New Left Review* 151: 44–73.

Timerman, Jacobo. *Preso sin nombre, celda sin número*. Buenos Aires: El Cid Editor, 1981.

Toro, Fernando de. "Griselda Gambaro o la desarticulación semiótica del lenguaje." Mazziotti 41–53.

162

Ure, Alberto. "Dejar hablar al texto sus propias voces." Mazziotti 13–23.

Varela-Cid, Eduardo, Luis Vicens. *La imbecilización de la mujer: Para Ti. Vosotras. Estudio de la ideología de las revistas femeninas en Argentina*. Buenos Aires: El Cid Editor, 1984.

Vargas-Llosa, Mario. "The Writer in Latin America." *They Shoot Writers, Don't They?* Ed. George Theiner. London: Faber and Faber, 1984. 161–71.

Waisman, Carlos H. "Argentina: Autarkic Industrialization and Illegitimacy." *Democracy in Developing Countries: Latin America*. Eds. Larry Diamond, Juan J. Linz and Seymour Martin Lipset. Boulder, Colorado: Lynne Rienner Publishers, 1989. 59–109.

Walsh, María Elena. Interview. "La madre de todas nosotras." *Alfonsina* 1 (Dec. 1983): 4–5.

Wandor, Michelène. *Carry On, Understudies: Theatre and Sexual Politics*. London: Routledge & Kegan Paul, 1986.

Weimer, Christopher B. "Gendered Discourse in Paloma Pedrero's *Noches de amor efímero*." *Gestos* 16 (Nov. 1993): 89–102.

Wolfe, Judy. "The Filmmaker and Human Rights." *Forbidden Films*. Toronto: Toronto Arts Group for Human Rights, 1984. 4–7.

Zatlin, Phyllis. "The Theater of Ana Diosdado." *Estreno* 3.1 (1977): 13–17.

_____. "Ana Diosdado and the Contemporary Theatre." *Estreno* 10.2 (1984): 37–40.

_____. "Feminist Perspectives on Selected Contemporary Spanish Plays." *The Minnesota Review* 26 (1986): 134–38.

Zito Lema, Vicente. "El oficialismo de *La historia oficial.*" *Madres de Plaza de Mayo* 1.6 (May 1985): 15.

Index